The Art of Sober Presents
Who Moved My Martini?

A common sense business minded tool kit to stop drinking and start living

Ryan P. O'Day
TheArtofSober.com

For my family.

Pretend you died today. What happens?

Let this concept really sink deep as you imagine the total number of final breaths you might have. Maybe you imagine a quick death that takes 12 seconds as your heart ceases and the lifeforce is pumped out into the ether, transferring energy into a different form.

Maybe you imagine the nightmare of drowning in a tidal riptide on your tenth anniversary with the love of your life, while your three children wave from the beach, smiling, shouting, unaware that you are not coming back.

Possibly, you are twenty-two, your knees crushed beneath the steering wheel of your new car on an off-ramp, struck head-on by a drunk driver traveling the wrong way up the on ramp. Crushed in between the airbag and seat with no possible way out. You burn alive for forty-three minutes. You convulse in agony, screaming for escape, your neck snapping under the strain. Extinguished much too soon. The driver of the other car naturally lives, while you die.

Pretend you die.

There is the emotional and business side of death. Things near you feel the pain the most. Things further away feel the pain less. Things not in your realm are not affected. Life will and does go on.

Now, let's die. Your old self needs to die. Not physically, but mentally. Your entire old self does not need to be destroyed, but parts of it must be shed and peeled away like dead bark. That is where not drinking begins. It must simply be allowed to die. Released and observed as the idea of it dissipates like cigar smoke in autumn air. Easier said than done. But you can start with some basic 'litmus tests' of things 'dying off' around you. Start by cleaning out a closet. Throw away what is not practical anymore. Try cleaning out your fridge of that nasty stuff you 'thought' you were going to eat to be more healthy but now has mold begging you to dump it into garbage. Throw that stupid piece of wood in your garage out. Stop fooling yourself and stop drifting into lives designed by other people. You have to do it for yourself, by yourself. You have to let pieces die off and concurrently create a new universe for yourself to live within. Within a quiet form of pandeism, repeat this: I am, and I was.

As each day comes to an end, people will either stick by you or leave you, in some fashion or another. Clinging to those already drifting away will cost you far more pain than it ever costs them. Just let them go. Misery. A wretched past life, but toast to your new you. Long live living if living can be sober. Alcohol betrays you. There is light, there is hope.

You must be the first to decide whether you stay with yourself or abandon yourself. So, now is the time to have a centuries old tradition of drinking die off with you, and be a first mover to get closer to those that are sticking with the current, alcohol drenched wretched you and leave those that are inclined to leave you anyways. You need to be in control of your universe, with gratitude.

Congratulations, you are now one of the 1% of the world that doesn't drink based on a religious belief. Ready?

.00002 - That's the number

Think about this: in the entertainment world, there may be one singer, or a band of five, on stage, and forty-five thousand people watching. Do the ratio math. It is truly insane. The ratio is staggering. That singer represents just 0.00002 of the population at a single stop. Multiply that across an entire tour, and the ratio shrinks even further. When you compare the people who act with the people who support them, the imbalance becomes unmistakable. Movie stars, celebrities, artists of all types, creators, CEOs - uniquely positioned personalities. Nearly every "top" individual is supported by thousands, sometimes hundreds of thousands, of others. The famous Jeff Bezos or Bill Gates has thousands of underlings that are propping them up to be the 'wealthiest' in the world. This concept of leverage is where your power begins. You are now your own CEO. While you may not have an army of employees under you, we want you to visualize having an army of supporting resources. Not just people, but activities, routines, beliefs, and goals. You make mistakes like any normal person, yet you can navigate through those miscalculations and propel yourself forward into positive territory with support from this army. You are about to make a massive bet on yourself and you can win it all!

Let it be known: the right path was never drinking in the first place. No one really teaches us that in school. Alcohol was most likely just put in front of you, and you drank. It is that simple. Every person who has had a drink has their 'first drink' story. Everyone. The United States law says you should wait until you are of the legal age of 21. England says 18 years old for drinking. Cultures vary. Some cultures by law let you marry a 14 year old - weird, but it's allowed in certain places in the world. Doesn't mean you HAVE to marry a 14 year old, it is simply allowed. Sick fucks if we do say so ourselves on that subject. We digress. This leads us to the discussion of culture and restrictions.

Restrictions, or self-imposed constraints, around drinking are plentiful. Subconsciously or not, you already know if you drink too much in certain settings, it will not be a good look, say a work function with your bosses. On the other hand, there seem to be no restrictions on drinking at a bachelorette party, lifting your shirt and showing off those boobies at the baseball game crowd. Why is that? Same person, two distinct outcomes. That's the power booze has over you. Don't get us wrong. Most guys like seeing a chick flash her boobs all day long. But really, your two kids don't want to hear about it on Monday at elementary school.

"Jimmy's Mom has some pepperoni sized nipples I hear, and some weird stretch marks on her stomach."

Alcohol as a concept is ingrained in our psyche so deeply that it allows varied behaviors to permeate, based purely on the consumption or even holding of it in our hand. Start to notice people around you. When there is no alcohol in the environment, they act their 'normal' self around you. But, once you place a drink in front of them, it's like a light switch. They act completely differently, sometimes even before taking 1 sip.

Alcohol is like Dr. Frankenstein moving the lever to 'on' and jolting you with a lightning bolt. You think you're smart when you drink? I got news for you, Coot, you are not smart. You're a fucking moron. Absolute moron. Harsh? We will be harsh from time to time in this body of work. We have to be. You may have a trigger that makes you think you are more interesting or smart, but we can assure you, it's not real. There is even a company that spent millions of dollars on marketing the most interesting man in the world because he drank their beer. Millions.

Save your embarrassment and if you cannot just be a member of the Irish Mafia by quitting drinking, start keeping a journal about your exploits, and reread after a month. Try to keep as much detail as possible. Write in your journal what happened to that ice cream sandwich you grabbed out of the freezer right before you went to bed but were derailed because you had to puke. Oh, we know what happened to it. It was melting on the bed and your wife climbed in and smushed the shit out of it, spreading it all over the sheets. What a sight to see at midnight! It looked like a tampon someone put up their ass, then proceeded to do their 2, and just left it behind. Heathens I tell you. Read your journal of drinking. Once you quit booze, you are part of the Irish Mafia. The world's best-kept society.

The Irish Mafia

The Irish Mafia is our brand and a universe. It is the group of folks that do not drink, but instead run the show. It is perceived that the Irish drink a lot. That may be so. The Irish Mafia doesn't drink. We exist to help people on their journey and to keep them focused on their "sober north" of the compass. We encourage you to take control of your journey and elevate yourself, at your own pace. Build your mental wealth. No one can take that away from you. We help where needed, keeping folks within their guardrails. Sometimes we are asked to hold someone more accountable. Other times, we are told to fuck off. Either way, we eventually reach an understanding and help move things forward. There are no coins, handshakes, or tattoos. You know one when you see one. They are sober - first and foremost.

We Moved Your Martini

The Art of Sober is moving your martini far away. How you move it is up to you. We will explore many variations to moving your martini in this handbook. We hope you find one or more methods to start with, eventually settling on a system that reliably gets you where you want to be: sober. At some point, you will simply be you—not "sober you," just you, without alcohol. Join this group and build a purposeful life in this regard and the rewards will far outweigh any riches you have ever achieved. You will unlock wealth in ways you may not comprehend right now.

Human wealth is not money. It is free time and the internal ability to rise above to make choices freely, not ones that handcuff you. In 6 months time, you will either have 6 months of excuses or 6 months of progress. Let us help you gain mental wealth. Be the person betting on themselves. Mental wealth is being able to manage your own self and also, if you decide, the ability to mentor others onto a more enlightened path without alcohol. Booze is a thief. Catch the thief, lock it away, rid yourself of the dangerous risk, and live carefree. Carefree, knowing you will not get a DUI on a first date, you will not manslaughter your little neighbor down the street as you come home at 7pm from a happy hour, blitzed on some rot gut shit tequila, or you will not pull into the garage too far and smash the shit out of your kids new bike. Carefree from booze is the Irish Mafia way.

Begin your journey with very small, incremental steps. We do not suggest trying to leapfrog into sobriety. Journaling is a powerful method to begin the strategy of going sober. If it takes you one day or one hundred days, journaling before you decide to quit will undoubtedly provide some interesting takes on events, if you are really truthful with it. Being truthful is a great power. Sometimes the truth will land you in hot water, and that's okay. That happens. Mistakes are to be learned from. Behavioral mistakes and misjudgments do happen, and they can be reckoned and reasoned with. No one is perfect, but striving to be truthful is pretty close to being perfect. Maybe you don't want to be a truth teller like your Mom is with you and the weight you've gained, but that's for another day. Be a truth teller to yourself first and foremost.

Tell yourself the truth. You can quit alcohol completely and we're here to help. You don't need to get a tattoo on your arm emblazoned with 'Truth Teller' but you should burn it in your brain nonetheless, nonstop. Calm conviction you can do sober. The Irish Mafia lives and dies by telling the truth. Not many can handle it, but the more people that realize it begin to understand the deeper meaning of life and actions. Truth is a mental wealth builder that wastes little time.

Tell yourself the truth. You can quit drinking. You can. It might be stepping into the unknown, but you know it is time. Make it your business. It pays very well. Along the way, you need to recalibrate and stop acting like middle management. You need to be the CEO of your life, not the middle manager of your life. Surrender the familiar for a life more authentic.

Whether you're an entrepreneur, a grocery bagger, a mechanic, a stay-at-home parent, a douchebag, or something else entirely, you should set goals. As you reach one goal, stack on another. Be sure to celebrate small wins along the way with purposeful gratitude. Then set higher goals, increased challenges, and overcome more lofty obstacles.

Let it be known: drinking is holding you personally back in ways you cannot imagine, until you cut it off and unleash that wasted time and energy. There are ideas of reference and delusions of reference. While the average person may not know the subtle differences, our basic take is the following, borrowing a bit from Carl Jung, Otto Fenichel, Jacques Lacan, and our good ol' boy, Freud, regarding alcohol;

You have a feeling people are talking about your alcoholism. This is the idea of reference. A stronger conviction that you think people are, in fact, talking about you elevates the idea to a delusion of reference. Simply put, you are delusional about your alcohol consumption whether people are talking about or not talking about your drinking. Alcoholism often causes a person, from time to time, to experience innocuous events or mere coincidences and believe them to have strong personal significance, the notion that everything you perceive in the world relates to your own destiny, usually in a net negative or hostile manner. To resist the idea that they are alcoholic, people convince themselves they are in control over their constitution. They aren't. That person simply does not want to give up alcohol. That is not for us to judge.

This may leave you thinking 'how can I win' against alcoholism. References of alcohol need to be detached, and this may take some time. Your frame of reference, your ideas of alcohol, have been, over time, turned into delusions of grandeur. The 'system' tricked you into thinking it is liquid fun, will get you laid, will reduce your stress, and so much more greatness. You have been relentlessly programmed from endless angles that alcohol is needed to do pretty much anything. They think you are stupid. Hiking? I need booze in the mountains. Football game? Booze makes it better. Just breathing? Take a sip between breaths. Hunting? Success comes from beer. Family time? Way better lubed up. Want to be a sophisticated gal about town? Drink a Cosmo. We can go on and on and on. They neatly packaged, marketed, and delivered it to you. Alcohol ads from the 50's - 80's were strong with subliminal imagery in ways you cannot even imagine. They invoked katathym-imaginative psychotherapeutic messaging. Their ideas have you engulfed in delusions that a cocktail is making you more sophisticated or that an expensive bottle of wine is really worth it (reference Holland Tulip Mania here or dot com bubble of 1999). Alcohol is fugazi. Good news for you from the Irish Mafia, it does not have to be a repeating circular event. You CAN get off the alcohol carousel ride. You are and you were.

That is easy enough for us to say, and we will get into the nuanced barbed wire of cutting off drinking, but trust us when we say it is holding you back. You could stop reading now, stop drinking now, and in 48 hours, your life will change right before your eyes just by not drinking. Drinking is that pervasive and mind melding both negatively and positively. Tune it out. It's like jumping from the first clunky steam car straight into a modern electric vehicle. Hard to imagine this until you experience it. Very hard to imagine if you cannot visualize a world where that COULD exist. That world DOES exist, you just have to get there. There is a world beyond the twilight zone of alcohol. As the saying goes, if you know, you know. You now know, but you do have to do some work. Once you are in the Irish Mafia, opportunities abound. You now know there is a world beyond alcohol. This is no secret being kept from you. It is there.

Drinking is not a goal or cool. It is glamorized, sort of, in many aspects of life. Booze is a product, plain and simple, that is heavily marketed. It has great profit margins and is easy to understand because of what it does. Alcohol transforms you into something you typically are not. Courageous, flirtatious, risk taker, and most likely above all, a dipshit. A gym can transform you, eating better food can transform you, religion can transform you - they are all marketed to you, but none are as easy as cracking open a bottle of beer or wine at 6:45p to "reward yourself" for doing whatever it is you think was hard that day. Boozing is not a goal we want anyone to strive for. Most think it is complementary to their goals. Now that is delusional.

I am learning guitar licks whilst drinking whiskey. Let's pause for a moment. Did it ever occur to you that in glamorizing the whiskey swilling raucous partying on stage by rock stars, it was really just tea in their bottles all along? Duped, right? You played right into it. Guided imagery. The rock star goes home after the show, sober. You, on the other hand, are emulating him later that night getting smashed after the concert thinking how great you will be if you ever learned how to really play that Stratocaster. As a girl, you might think it's cool and, hey, you really know how to play the skin flute, so maybe you got a future!

You think you have a problem, go find a bigger problem. Move your martini. Move it far away. The concept we will talk about next can be summed up nicely as the "Marginalized Martini Movement" action.

Practice this concept if you cannot just cut booze out 100%. In fact, this method works well for almost anything you want to reduce or stop doing 100%. Funny side note, want to stop dating or go celibate for 6 months, go hit on the uglies. It will no doubt backfire, as they do not get any attention and will be all over you! But the cold reality is, those folks are probably the most genuine out there and may make you the happiest, so don't judge uglies and get to work. We digress. When it comes to reducing your drinking, one method is to slowly reduce your standards of the quality of booze. The headaches become more gargantuan, the taste is awful, and the weight you will gain is insurmountable. You'll be a total lard ass fat fuck in no time, just one more thing you will have to work on. Let's avoid decreasing your standards and just get to not drinking at all. You can do it. Here are some pointers.

Make the accessibility of the item increasingly more difficult to obtain. It 'should' reach a point where the difficulty to obtainability is so high, your effort/reward just isn't there. Here is the added element most people don't add into the mix when trying to quit. As you move your martini further away, replace it with something that gets closer to you. You are simply replacing one for the other. In this instance, in the early stages, club soda is currently furthest away, martini closest. As you proceed through space and time, club soda becomes closer, and the martini further away. You're naturally a lazy fuck, so you will think you are winning when you go for the club soda because it is so close. You are winning. But alas, humans naturally like to cheat at things (don't say you don't, that is bullshit) as long as it doesn't elasticate past their belief systems, so they will say fuck it and go for the martini over the club soda, cheating on themselves. This type of relapse causes the problem. They were so close, now they are back to square one. They are literally hurting themselves the most when cheating in this manner. With this type of cheating, they are hitting the proverbial "button" that doesn't kill them, but not making any meaningful progress towards their goal of quitting drinking. What button are we talking about, you ask?

This is loosely based on a 1960s experiment people participated in that administered a shock on people by hitting a button or not. Here is the button of shock concept reimagined and applied to alcohol and yourself.

Here is the gist; if you hit the button, you get mildly shocked. If you don't hit the button, you are told someone else gets shocked almost to the point of death but the experiment is over and you are no longer shocked. If you shock yourself, the experiment carries over to the next day.

You don't want to seriously hurt anyone, so you choose to hit the button, suffering your shock. Reality begins to be lost. The other side of that button is faceless, unidentified. Just delusional you and the button. You eventually become numb to the shock and just repeat it over and over and over, thinking that at least no one is getting really hurt, so how bad can it be.

You really do not have proof of or know if anyone would really get shocked badly if you didn't hit your button, so you just blindly continue to shock yourself, assuming what you are told by the institution would happen is indeed the set up.

You suffer your continual daily shock without question and seem pleased no one else is getting shocked badly. You are not questioning the experiment, authority or institution administering your experiment. You are just showing up daily to carry it out. This is basically alcohol wrapping its grip around you. This is the authority of alcohol. If you knew it was only your drinking habit that would end, would you continue to shock yourself? You must risk something to personally free yourself. Many people shock themselves daily and they control the button. But today is a new day, and the authority of alcohol over you needs to stop. Once it stops, you no longer have to continually shock yourself. Game over. Alcohol as the institution does not hold authority over you. Thank you, guy in the experiment room, I would like to leave now and start my new life.

You are breaking out of your own paradigm by shifting from blind complacency to letting something be shocked. Do not let alcohol be the authority to which you are living day to day. What matters is YOU, and you are no longer shocking yourself daily with a martini, glass of wine, or beer. For your greater good, you need to stop shocking yourself. This is not Schrödinger's cat theory on quantum mechanics and observations on whether your drinking exists or doesn't exist inside the box that no one has opened. You need to pick your observation. You are either drinking, or you are not. No funny business. Let's stop being a middle manager of your life and begin acting like a CEO, or the President of You, Inc.

First steps: The Why

Why does not drinking feel taboo? Guilt. People who don't drink rarely waltz around asking others why they do or don't drink. They typically clam up. STOP clamming up. Just order your preferred drink. At this stage of your life, you are the 0.000022%. The drinkers are the watchers - the fans, the folks that just can't seem to figure out how to get where you are. Maybe they do. Maybe they don't. That is not for us to cast about. Not drinking takes less effort than trimming bushes, washing your car, vacuuming, or building a campfire. Simply choose not to drink. This may sound implausible. It isn't.

The Art of Sober observes that much of the world treats drinking as part of the activity, not the main event, while others see it as the event itself. Adjusting your perceptions of where alcohol fits into the schema of your life is a critical first step. Stop for a few minutes and really just think back over the last two to three years of any events you might have attended. Ask "WHY?" 5 times as to why there was booze present. By the 5th WHY you will have your answer, and it will most likely not be mind blowing or life changing. The answer may be so mundane that it barely registers, it should just make you shrug your shoulders like Atlas. We will delve into this exercise of asking WHY much deeper later, but for now, let's take some basic examples as a simple exercise to start your ball rolling;

Why was there booze there? Because I was at a football game. Answered in the first WHY. Let's get a little harder.

Why was there booze there? Because I was at an absolutely insufferable art gallery opening in North Chicago and the only way to get anyone in the fucking door was by offering free rosè. Done.

Why was there booze there? Because it was Thanksgiving with extended family. Fair enough.

Now let us flip the authoritative word 'WHY' on its head. Asking WHY 5 times to get to a root cause of why booze was present is one use of the exercise. Now, we will ask a more vigorous anchored 'why' - WHY will you quit booze? You may ask it 5 times, but you may only need 1.

Going deeper into the 4th and 5th WHY really anchors your Why. 5 Whys to quit, for example;

1) My kids. To be more present at their sporting events of soccer (organized running)
2) So I can really assess their skills and react to their fragile, young emotions in real time
3) My kids should learn confidence, emotional management, and lessons in both defeat and victory, via soccer as the tool
4) Not everyone wins or loses, but it will teach them deeper levels of humility and gratitude to develop methods of management in the outcome based on team and individual efforts.
5) I see soccer as a teachable building block—an early lesson in effort, teamwork, and consistency for my 8 year old to realize hours invested in practice, side by side with teammates will eventually provide a solid foundation for being an excellent father, husband and all around genuine human being in their community. He will be great one day because of the first of my 5 Whys - being present.

Notice how this anchor leads to a deeper, more meaningful outcome. All too often, people are surface oriented and only see 1 dimension, or layer of a situation. When you hear the phrase 'let's unpack this,' they are not talking luggage. It refers to how what is 'in the box' is all interconnected. Unpacking the WHY at least 5 times helps develop a deeper connection to the subject matter. Again, it might only be 2-3 levels, but if you keep digging, you will find it can get more meaningful, and possibly, more complex.

Learn what your whys for not drinking are and use that as a starting point. They may change over time and become more robust or less inclusive, that is fine. Life is fluid and priorities change. Start somewhere. It might be as simple as wanting to sleep better, save $10 a day, or free up time to work out 30 minutes longer. Skip happy hour. Trust us - it's rarely a happy hour. It is typically a bitch session hour. If they really called it what it was, it would be 'misery hour' for so many folks. Settle on at least one WHY. We will discuss methodology in more depth later. Let's continue.

Booze is The Machine

Booze is perceived as the grease between the cogs of life. You need to stop that way of thinking. Break that monotony - and authority - of alcohol today. You need to see it for the machine it is, and you must rage against that machine and get angry. It's almost as if booze IS the 1984 Orwellian socio-economic fabric of your daily existence. Watching over you, controlling you, scolding you if you fail to imbibe. The world has you thinking if you don't support the all-puissant booze, you will be nobody. The Irish Mafia declares it's time to suspend your belief in the religion of rye and seek the true elements of the periodic table of life. Your personal periodic table allows you to coexist with others and form new, healthier bonds. We think you will find that once you quit booze, your core properties should align. Fair warning: do not be evangelical in your newfound path. No one can hear you scream in space.

Just as few people care about your day at work, fewer still care about your sober journey. On the surface, this is harsh. Of course some DO care about your progress. The ones that are immediately affected will, at the onset, care. But do not expect constant 'congratulations' from people. It just won't happen. You need to congratulate YOU. For some, being sober is a constant battle; for others, less so. At every moment, it is just you. Sure, joining a group can help with shared circumstances and aligned experiences. But here is the hemorrhoid. While 'groupings and gatherings' got you hooked on booze, it is ONLY you and your most trusted, closest folks that will get you off of it and keep you off of it. A rag-tag bunch of people will be in a room doing what they do, but they don't pay your rent, buy your gas, or wipe your ass. It is only you. Some of you reading this may not even have close, trusted people. That is no bueno, but you can do it. Look in the black mirror. You'll get there. Repeat after us: I am, and I was.

Condition your mind and your muscle memory to understand that sober is ultimately on you. This mindset removes some crutches you could potentially face in the future. You are in this for yourself, but not by yourself.

Your immediate loved ones typically have a vested interest in your success, but in the end, your quitting should not interfere with their choice to keep drinking. Each person has their own journey. You are on your journey. Try not to take away from their experiences. Let them enjoy their wins, night out, birthday and more. They may never realize how profoundly alcohol shapes their lives. Like many habits or successes, you just need to hunker down and do it yourself. You will reward yourself along the way for the little and big milestones and victories. Each victory builds on the last, and even small discoveries begin to compound into mental health and wealth. Let the people around you coexist with you in their manner. Don't even mention that you're reducing your drinking or that you're sober. They will find out at some point. Move your needle. Increase your voltage. Do not let others reduce it.

Routines

You certainly have a routine. Study how booze plays into that routine. Now remove the booze and examine what time, energy, and attention are freed up. Relationships should grow more meaningful, efficiencies should increase, and the quality of your life should improve. Write it down if you have to. Track the time spent shopping for alcohol, the money spent, and the activities built around it. Some rationalize it as a hobby - collecting whiskeys, wines or other libations, or simply an interesting thing similar to eating. OK. We challenge you to go to an art store with the same enthusiasm. You will most likely collapse like a kid with low blood sugar, wake up, and start crying in the corner. Art supply stores are no joke.

A Typical Saturday

Here's a typical summer Saturday for a Joe Six-Pack beer guy:

> Well, I am preparing for a BBQ, so I need choice meat, delicious side items, favorite craft beer, some seltzers, ice, limes, that one BBQ rub my wife nags me about, 4 cigars that I have no clue what I am buying, ice (again), and chips. You will undoubtedly purchase the worst chips out there, usually tortilla ones. Newsflash, NO ONE likes those You'll forget anything about a dessert.

Your routine as a newly sober person can still look similar to this, but with some minor tweaks. After all, you are entertaining.

Sure, you might want to drink something besides plain water, so go ahead and splurge. Just tell your guests to bring what they want to drink, or be a great host and inquire what they would like and buy their alcohol for them as a host. Just because you do not drink anymore doesn't mean you are cut off from the world. You will still be present. In fact, your version of sobriety may become something others respect. Just don't shove it on people. You mind your business, and if they are interested, you can discuss aspects of your journey. Most do not even bother asking. They are too afraid to ask. Some folks reading this might be appalled that a newly sober person is even considering alcohol near them. We are not saying to haphazardly be around alcohol, but it is possible. Gauge your level of comfort, or don't entertain folks. It is very possible to host parties sober. It happens.

We're not shy about offending people, but not over quitting alcohol. Be confident in your decision to quit and discuss it with conviction. You are being called to quit. Do it with inspiration, clarity, and destiny. Most folks are not going to berate you for not drinking. You will be pleasantly surprised to know that you are maybe even triggering folks to reconsider their relationship with alcohol. If a person does indeed berate or disqualify your efforts, lose their contact info. If they ask why you are not drinking, be truthful, but don't drone on. You are strong. Similar to any effective business meeting, make the time and topic clear, to the point, and decisive. This is no different. Treat every interaction like an important meeting and you will find your 'explanation' time frame will collapse into a concise 15-30 second quip when needed. You will gain a keen insight into who is supportive or dismissive of you. Again, most people do not dwell on your life decision of not drinking. In your own mind, you should not dwell on it either. These people have their own problems. Here are some quick comeback quips to help you out;

"I've moved on from distractions, it has helped me professionally and personally."

"I'm putting my money into the stock market. Look at alcohol prices? Put that into the stock market and 10 years from now, a massive house remodel is coming my way!"

"I find I am a hell of a lot healthier and living an extra 2-4 years is worth it in the long run for me today, who knows what the future holds!"

Many chumps may reply with an under-educated anecdote along the lines of a 'relatable' story of a person who didn't drink, yet still suddenly died at 46. The old 'relatable story time.' Many people do it to convey understanding of your situation. Of course, they cannot truly understand your unique situation. That is OK. Just listen and be attentive. That is actually one of the mechanisms to a more solid foundation of soberness and just being a better, more present person.

Want to really chooch someone, just quip back with "Well, I can tell you if I was drinking, you would definitely look a whole lot better, but I'm not drinking.' BOOM! Or just skip it entirely and nod your head, roll your eyes, and realize they are not on your level. Low voltage people.

Your truth of why you do not drink will morph into the most real component in your life eventually. It may take longer than you want, but you will get there. You will second guess yourself, maybe 'fall off the wagon' a few times trying to quit, make jokes about it, or just shy away from the subject and events in general. Despite the bumps along the way, keep moving forward. Most people are straight up awkward and are not experienced enough to dance around what is perceived to be a 'touchy' subject. Anyone can overcome this by being confident. It can be learned. Your ability to get ahead of the potential awkwardness of the sober topic will help you. Conversely, you can be silent and let them squirm in their awkwardness - either way is great, it just depends on your sense of humor and ability to be silent.

The truth as to why you quit drinking is personal and may be a touchy subject. Maybe not as touchy as why you chose to be Mormon, Baptist or a Scientologist. The Irish Mafia suggests you thicken up your armor and not really give a shit what other people think of you - they are going to form their own opinions regardless of what you say or do, no matter what. You will barely change anyone's mind about you. Might as well put some footnotes up their ass for contemplation of their assessment of you. There are plenty of inspirational quotes and sayings that you will come across. Social media is littered with one liners of inspiration. Find one or two quotes that resonate with you at times in your journey, ignite that curiosity of what is down your path, and keep moving. We think the ontology of a person on an intentional journey is more forthcoming and explorative than a person who is a lump on a fucking log stuck in their daily routine. For example, having two competing thoughts in your head at one time is healthy. Believing one truth and never willing to listen to another perspective is the death knell. Ultimately, you should not care what other people think. It gets you nowhere in life, especially in this journey.

Breakthrough thoughts will continue to emerge. Embrace the Eleatic principle of ontology—"power is the mark of being." Because you possess causal influence, particularly over your sobriety, your agency is real. Let that principled sense of being guide you toward building mental wealth.

Allow your ontology to be disrupted, because once you quit drinking, you are going to go on a rampage of newfound emboldenment that no one can stop. You might walk around and under your breath just start calling people wicked names, pointing out faults, seeing things for how stupid and innocuous they really are, judging dogs, cats, kids, parks, schools, cars, bikers, joggers, toddlers and fast food joints like a motherfucker. Careful not to judge people on God given traits such as height or size of their schnoz. God brought them into the world as a midget - you cannot mock that. God. did not bring them in with stupid tattoos and piercings in their nose - have at it! DO IT. That is part of the process. Just don't go hog wild and tell everyone on the mountain your opinions, but unleash your internal free flow of ideas. Noticing the world around you is ok and healthy.

Once you realize how actually stupid some stuff is in the world, you will start seeing mindless sheep glued to entertainment and attractive nuisances on many levels. You will get to the grocery store and wonder WHY in the absolute world are there so many varieties of BBQ sauces, shampoos, toilet papers, hot dogs, breads, yogurts and frozen corn. Ask WHY 5 times, you will find the truth, and it is truly as lame as you think it is. We do not live in modern times because of today's advanced technology. We live in modern times because it is the 'present' time. Modernity is a loosely defined concept delineating a number of societal, economic and ideological features. You are in your modern time. Technology does not equate to modernity. In the metal ages 3,600 BCE, when metal was being forged into tools, weapons, and household items, it was technology, and because it was the present, it was, by default, the modern age at that time. Every forward point in life is 'modern' so we suggest you live in YOUR modern age. Technology does not dictate modernity.

We posit that *control* over oneself is the ultimate version of "modern" to strive for. The mind is the ultimate technical tool. Having a grasp and level of control over that is, in our definition, pure modern living. The ability to differentiate risks and rewards, dress yourself accordingly, be polite, wipe your ass, not eat ducks you found at the park, etc. are all benefits of well conceived thoughts that keep you modern. You could theorize that many activities that exist today have evolved from past modern times. Folks engage in past modern behaviors such as archery, billiards, reading, gardening, wood whittling, music, painting, etc. They are also, by default, using their mind in the present, thus conducting, by default, modern hobbies.

While some of this may not make sense because you're not mentally there yet, think of this as it relates to your relationship with alcohol;

Drinking, either cathartically by itself in solitude staring at a wall or up into space or a companion to any activity, does not elevate the experience of the modern activity you are engaged in. Try not to argue that 'drinking' in itself is a hobby. It is an accomplice to a hobby. Beer 'brewing' and winemaking might make the cut, but we will place that in the file of 'reeks of dorky desperation' and 'tastes like complete dogshit' file. Drinking de-modernizes your activity and dilutes the importance of it. Having alcohol present while you paint may sound 'fun' and 'social' while you're painting some stupid sunrise over the water, Bob Ross knock off thing at a "Paint and Pinot" birthday party instead of sitting in front of a TV, but the reality is, you are wasting a slice of your life away because the alcohol will undoubtedly interrupt the natural flow. Drinking during this activity will lead you to make off-color comments to your kids, compare yourself to other parents, think you are not fitting in, or not really even give two shits what other people think. You will have all of these thoughts and more, instead of just trying to complete a cool painting with your sibling, son, or daughter at the Paint and Pinot birthday party you are attending. Being in the moment is modern. Be modern. Be in the moment.

Once you stop getting buzzed, your life should become simpler, more modern, and more streamlined. Way simpler. You won't care about all the noise and clutter. They cannot fool you anymore. You will have a slower paced existence, not coddled by invasive marketing and messaging coming at you from every single angle, including friends, family, TV, radio, phone apps, and more. You are cool, you don't need to be told you have to have a certain item to be cool. That liquid fun is not liquid fun.

The messaging noise is relentless. You buy into their messaging because you want to be somebody. When you stop this madness, you ARE somebody. You now control your mind, uncluttered by visions of grandeur. Modern. You might finally realize the picture of the Big Mac™ on the billboard does not look like what you get served. Once you have internalized the Big Mac™ Marketing Machine, everything typically starts to fall into place. You might have realized this years ago, but you just accepted it as is. It stopped there. You took another sip and just figured 'that's the life of a west side Big Mac™ eater, eating what they give me' bullshit.

Let's dig a bit deeper. The Art of Sober offers a lens through which to better understand sobriety: ontology. Ontology, in general, is the philosophical study of being. Ontology employs diverse methods of inquiry into existence itself, including persons, numbers, colors, and objects. This is a fascinating realm to explore further if you choose to do so. For our purposes here, we'll focus on social ontology as a key framework for achieving and maintaining sobriety. After all, it takes a village, and you want to be in the best possible village in order to succeed and thrive in sobriety.

Your primary ontological dependencies—what you rely on to function—will shift dramatically once you stop drinking. This is a critical element of sobriety that you, and only you, can navigate. Let's clarify what we at The Art of Sober mean by ontological dependence and its relationship to alcohol.

An entity is ontologically dependent on another entity if the first entity cannot exist without the second entity. Basically, an alcoholic cannot exist without alcohol. In practical terms, addiction creates the belief that one cannot exist without the addictive item. An entity is ontologically independent if it does not depend on anything else, meaning that it is fundamental and can exist on its own. You desire to be ontologically independent.

The next step is the ontological commitment to sobriety. An ontological commitment refers to what a person believes truly exists. For instance, a person who believes in God has an ontological commitment to God. In your case, a person who believes in being sober therefore has an ontological commitment to their sober self.

Finally, let's move to social ontology, which examines the social world and the entities that arise out of social interaction. A primary concern of social ontology is social groups, whether or not they exist (and if so, in what way), and if so, how they differ from any given collections of people. You certainly have some sort of social group, a cohort, beyond your family. This may include co-workers, friends, golf buddies, card playing groups, etc. This group has evolved, expanded, and contracted over time. It is a type of living organism. Your social ontological grouping is affectionately and simply referred to as your social reality. Philosophers such as Alfred Schütz have fleshed this out as far back as the 1930s. This work matters because it can become a pillar of sobriety, helping you dissect your world more deliberately. In 1932, Schutz's efforts resulted in his first published book, Der sinnhafte Aufbau der sozialen Welt ('The Meaningful Structure of the Social World') which was published in English as The Phenomenology of the Social World.

Schutz's main area of concern was the ways in which people grasp the consciousness of others while living within their own streams of consciousness. A great deal of his work deals with the "lifeworld," in which people create a social reality under the constraints of preexisting social and cultural factors and structures. He was very focused on the "dialectical relationship between the way people construct social reality and the obdurate social and cultural reality that they inherit from those who preceded them in the social world."

Schutz is also known for his belief that humans attempt to typify everything; i.e., to categorize people and things to better understand them within the context of society. He believed that the various typifications we use inform how we understand and interact with people and objects in the social world.

Now let's bring these philosophical concepts into context. The marketing, friend groups, activities, and hobbies you consume or have forced on you have a massive impact on the above philosophical positions. Your lifeworld is an existence of meaning that comes into play, yet most people simply accept their world as it is and never second guess the concept or problem of meaning. You play cards because you enjoy it. You golf, knit, garden, play sports because you enjoy it. You drink because you drink. Now, you are actively pursuing not drinking to not drink. This is the Yin and Yang—the interaction of opposing forces—forming a new order in your life as defined by Tao. You are creating a new sober social reality that is on the horizon of the direct experience of soberness.

These are centuries-old teachings meeting your modern life and times. Be modern in your intentional thoughts. As a matter of course, downtime and recharging is critical as well. We will get into allostatic recharge and energies later. For now, the Irish Mafia wants you to suspend your current beliefs for a bit of time, allow ancient thoughts to freely flow through your mind, and visualize singular parts of your journey you can more easily begin with and manage, reinforcing your ultimate effort to stop drinking.

Now that we have determined to proverbially die, have joined the elite group called The Irish Mafia, identified at least one real truth to our 'why' of not drinking and realize we have a sober north compass to guide us, let's get to it. A question you might be asking yourself after a few pages is why should you trust this particular author on this subject matter. What authenticity does the author have? Why did this clown write a book - profit, ego, posterity? Does he really want to help me, is it self serving, etc. etc. FAAAHK! Stop with all the questions, dear reader. It's basic: going sober requires, for a lot of folks, tools. Some need more tools than others. You might want to Fahrenheit 451 this book, or place it in some sort of shrine - your call. Either way, the author has a history to assist in your self performed assessment of your relationship with alcohol to help you get sober. Let's rock.

Bare knuckle truth is what people want, and modern living is telling the truth. Far too many folks bullshit or put on facades. Not the Irish Mafia. If you fake it, we break it. So let's break some perceptions and forge a new reality. You are not alone if you fucked up. We are all humans living in our own modern Xanadu-esque versions of ourselves. But for the love of God, do not walk around thinking you are the best parent / dog or cat parent ever, even if you do not drink. No one is. Lest ye who judge, go for it. A well regarded concept is 'getting it out there' as a coping mechanism. Here we go. Let's get it out there. You will read this book, march forward to your Mother or Father and get your story out there. Lose your inhibitions and be the sober soldier you were meant to be. Don't fuck it up, Chappy!

Let us dissect ontology and alcohol in a different format for readers:

Ontology (A Useful Lens for Sobriety)

Ontology is the branch of philosophy concerned with *being*—what exists, what depends on what, and what can stand on its own.

At first glance, this may sound abstract. It isn't. Ontology offers a practical definitive baseline to understanding your relationship with alcohol.

Ontological Dependence

An entity is *ontologically dependent* if it cannot exist without something else.

In addiction, alcohol becomes that "something else." Not biologically, but psychologically and socially. Life begins to feel organized around it, such as events, relationships, routines, and identity. Sobriety begins when this dependence is questioned.

Ontological Independence

An entity is *ontologically independent* if it can exist on its own.

The goal of sobriety is ontological independence: becoming a person whose sense of self, meaning, and agency no longer rely on alcohol. You are still you, only now, you exist without that dependency on alcohol.

Ontological Commitment

An ontological commitment refers to what you believe truly exists and matters. For example:

- A religious person has an ontological commitment to God.
- A person pursuing sobriety has an ontological commitment to their sober self.

This commitment shapes decisions, priorities, and behavior often quietly, but powerfully.

Social Ontology

Social ontology examines how groups form and how social realities are created.

Your social world—friends, coworkers, routines, traditions—did not appear by accident. It evolved. Drinking often plays a structural role in that world. When you stop drinking, your **social reality will change**. Some relationships strengthen. Others fade. New ones form. This is not a failure, it is a natural ontological shift.

Philosopher **Alfred Schütz** described this as the *lifeworld*: the shared reality we inherit and reinforce through daily interaction. Sobriety reshapes that new lifeworld.

Why This Matters

Sobriety isn't just about removing alcohol. It's about reorganizing what you depend on, what you commit to, and how you exist among others.

That's ontology working quietly in the background as your life changes.

Let us now officially begin. This book took 37 years to write, we hope you find the tools beneficial in your journey to you becoming you.

1. The Initial Estimation
The Catalyst and the Required Maintenance

Let's get started on a few different philosophies, beliefs, ideas and concepts of identity.

When an author or thinker has contributed an idea, we aim to give proper credit. From time to time, we will highlight these folks and their contributions to your journey. You may find a connection and further delve into their teachings as part of your unique journey. The credit given is their social currency, and later we will teach you the value of your social currency.

When it comes to substance abuse, think about the following statements from an author that specializes in philosophical uncertainties.

"If you change your mind too frequently, it suggests you did not think carefully before forming an opinion.

If you never change your mind, it suggests intellectual dishonesty.

There are two kinds of people: those who try to win, and those who try to win arguments. They are never the same.

A Stoic transforms fear into prudence, pain into transformation, mistakes into initiation, and desire into undertaking."
— Nassim Nicholas Taleb

Being honest or dishonest with yourself is a major decision and will determine how far you do or do not leap forward in your progress of combating the substance. Frame every decision as if you are at war with the issue and you will think more than passively. If you are playing the 'game' of quitting, play the fucking game, but on a level it cannot beat you. Play 5-D chess, not checkers. Play to win, not for a participation trophy. Play as if your life depended on it, because, as cliche as it sounds, your life pretty much depends on it. Are you trying to win, or win the argument? Finding your catalyst for quitting can be daunting and full of self-doubt.

Find Your Catalyst

You may not see the pathway or a need to quit now because you are maybe under 32 years old, work out 3 days a week (leg day, what a joke), wake up at 6am, golf 1 Men's league day a week, chew gum while you drink your Bud Light, and do not smoke. Newsflash: all of your actions resonate and each action becomes another proverbial brick in the wall. If charted, your habits break down into small percentages of each day. Breaking that day down is daunting, but try to journal and pie graph it some time. Mark how many activities also include alcohol. You will be stunned and amazed at the overlap. Many folks are living the 'long game' of 'set it and forget it' with alcohol. It is just there as an ingrained part of the fabric of being. It is hard to just let that go. Interestingly enough, the word catalyst comes from the Greek word kataluein, meaning "loosen" or "untie". You are searching for something to begin loosening the grip alcohol has on you.

What will one or two beers a day, every so often, really matter? In the long run, that person never binge drinks (so they say). They spend energy keeping an even keel. These folks often say 'I have a healthy relationship with alcohol' to justify it. "I only kick my dog in the ribs one time per month to show him who is boss" type of people. The eighth wonder of the world is compounded interest. In this case, your drinks compound over time. Not so wonderful. You will undoubtedly find yourself making more time for the drinks than other things. Over time the drink creeps up on you. Eventually you prioritize the 2+ drinks over spending time with your spouse or kids, or getting to that project. These are such subtle shifts in behavior that typically occur over years, that you do not notice them, but from an outsider looking in, they can spot it immediately. It doesn't take a mental giant to realize some fat asses probably not only drink too much, but also eat too much. Combined, you are just hurting yourself. Alas, let's stick to the booze. If you have eating issues, that is another topic unto itself, but get some help there too.

One possible catalyst to get you started might be the idea that empty calories provide no intrinsic value to you. Drinking booze is literally drinking empty calories with basically zero health benefit. Beer, wine, vodka, etc. all have calories. You justify drinking vodka with club soda because it has less calories. Fact check, it does, but it still has calories and all the ancillary problems that go along with it. We are not here to preach, but rather to help you find your catalyst and maintenance for quitting your habits. Some will justify the benefits of drinking. Let them have that, they will realize soon.

Let's pause and make finding your catalyst a little bit easier. Knowledge of catalysts is great, but we need applied knowledge. What you do with that catalyst.

You know how you label and judge things? Try doing that to yourself. It can be daunting at first, unless you are a self deprecating fool by nature (seek professional help). Look at yourself AGAINST yourself and ask what can be improved. Not fixed, improved. We in the Irish Mafia are ultra sensitive to things you cannot fix that God gave you - height, skin tone, size of feet, etc. If you are a midget, this exercise should take half the time. We kid. Things you were born with, do not analyze. You are great just the way you are in that regard. Never criticize someone for something such as the nose given to them at birth. Maybe you went ahead and started messing with the perfect machine that is your body, that is different. Maybe remove those stupid piercings you got when you were 22? It's costly to remove those ignorant tattoos you got in your 'angry at my parents for loving me too much' phase, so skip that. Get a fucking haircut too. You have more chins than a Chinese phone book? Write it down if you want to work on it, but don't then look at the back of your neck, that'll make you cry. If it looks like a package of hot dogs, oy vey. If you want to fix your posture, get whiter teeth, grow a beard, or have clean fingernails, write it down and let's make it a goal. Stop being lazily unshaven on your face or if a female, your legs. For fucks sake stop wearing a baseball hat everywhere, including out to dinner at the table. Fucking take it off. If it is backwards, even worse. Are you a 9 year old latchkey kid trying to look 21 to buy a pack of Kool's? No one gives a shit if your hair is thin. No one is asking you to wear a button down collar. If a girl is wearing a hat, it's fashion. Guys? You're not fashion. Take a long inventory of your overall well being, appearance and presentation you provide to the world. No one is asking you to be cookie cutter. You are unique and special, just like everyone else. Find your 'you' and own it.

Develop your personal traits into strengths, divide out the weaknesses, acknowledge them, but do not dwell on them. You're fat and ugly? That is ok. Not everyone thinks you are. Self confidence is part of the transition. Do not let someone push you around. You can begin to lose weight, eat better, and stop drinking all at the same time. Daunting? Yes. Doable? Yes. Will it transform your life in ways you cannot imagine? Absolutely. Cut your greasy head of hair and viola, you are starting to get not ugly! We posit it is worth it to go to a reputable salon or barber and let them have creative freedom. A new you as it were. Bold moves will make you more fortunate, although you may not believe it, or think you can do it. Fortune favors the bold. We cannot stress that enough. Confidence is synthetic. Why do some people have confidence and others do not? Simple. They tried, and they do not care what others think. The worst outcome is hearing "no." If you are aware of your limits at a particular time, that is your confidence. Go to that level, try, and either succeed or fail at that moment. Then, try again & again. This skill set will eventually turn into a trait that will make you unstoppable. Own your destiny. Be confident with gratitude and people will be magnetized.

For example, fishing. It is perhaps the #1 most mundane, boring hobby on the planet to many folks. That is a perspective. But, let's break it down. It really is the #1 most important skill set in the world, without a doubt. Like being sober, it all resides in your ontology: your frame of reference.

If your outlook and opinion on fishing is based on experiences at Lake Michigan, standing off the pier in Kenosha, Wisconsin, at 5 a.m. in a 42° drizzle, and you didn't enjoy it because you grew up "doing it" and were dragged there by your grandpa, then your viewpoint might be valid. But, replace you with a kid with an absentee or dead father, and you may have another view of fishing with your grandpa. A different perspective. That is one type of fishing. You tossed them back. Maybe the point of that 'fishing' was spending time and you forgot or retained many of the life lesson's Grandpa went over with you, Oh La La.

Let's move to the southern United States. Now you are fishing for catfish to feed the family. Fishing is no longer a hobby, but a way of life. Go to coastal Florida and fish for Square Grouper. You are in a completely different bracket of fishermen there. Head to Maine, and you are no longer fishing just for fish, but also harvesting lobster. Whilst a person might think fishing is boring, or not their thing, it is an activity many engage in for their reasons. As being sober, it may not be everyone's thing, but many engage in being sober for various reasons. It is no one's business why you are or want to be sober, you just do it. Just don't fish for compliments.

There is someone for everyone out there if that is what you are looking for. Stop going to your dog or cat for affirmation, they will lick your face no matter how many ugly sticks you hit on the way down the ugly tree. Just own it and realize - you are NOT ugly. You have something to offer the world and you need to simply adjust your frame of reference to find a new garden from which to grow. It is amazing how many before and after photos of drinkers showcase a massive transformation of a person. It truly is mind blowing. It happens over time, but it can happen if you focus and work on it. Nothing is typically completed in a few hours or a day except sometimes massive stock losses at the New York Stock Exchange. Trees can be transplanted to thrive more in a new environment - the same for you. Your catalyst should be simple and one or two sentences as to WHY you want to quit drinking and abusing. We will not suggest any sample catalysts more than we previously did, but the author's catalyst was simple:

Better and deeper presence and relationship with wife and two kids, and extended family.

Your catalyst is allowed to change as well. It doesn't need to be carved in stone, boxing you in. It may need to change as your social ontology morphs into new territory. Let's say your circumstances change, your catalyst can change. In fact, it is probably healthy to review every so often what your catalyst is as you move forward in life. Today your circumstances might be X situation. But shit, say you inherit $848,000.00. Now your situation has changed. Your new situation might be not to blow it all on being sober in a strip club in 7 months. Funny thing about those strip clubs. You get fucked, but you don't get laid. Life changes for you sometimes, you can certainly change with it. In fact, if life didn't change, it would suck. We would still be stuck in the caveman days grunting and banging rocks on walls, picking ticks off dicks. Guess where the first 'purple nurple' or 'titty twister' came from? Research the first caveman getting a tick off of a female. Change happens whether you like it or not. Embracing a newfound change to your catalyst to affect you positively is critical in your everyday journey, your growth and formative behaviors. You never stop learning and that leads to changing. The day you stop learning, you are dead. D.E.A.D.

If you are a younger college kid that is reading this, you are in the smartest group out there. We should hire you now while you know everything. Finding your catalyst may seem more difficult, but it isn't. This demographic is just coming out of the stage of being typically spoonfed BS their entire young lives by parents that aren't even most likely qualified to have kids themselves due to their mental immaturity and own vices to overcome. Go look into the parents medicine cabinet, do you have 3 hours to write down each prescription? Carpal tunnel of the wrist here we come. The younger set of kids get to a level of higher education or trade school and into a larger pool of social ontology and the majority of them all think the same thing - my parents are idiots, until they aren't.

Why are kids like this?

They go through the education, and come out knowing principles, but not practice. They have knowledge, which informs them, but typically not applied knowledge, which transforms them..

They quickly expect to get what their parents have. It typically doesn't happen for years. So younger kids reading this, you have a ways to go in the practicality of life, but the fact that you are at least opening ANY book about drinking means one thing, you are considering not doing it or wanting to quit. Sober curious. That is a massive mark of maturity. Combine that with not wearing that hat or hoodie everywhere, and now we are talking game changing. Moving on.

Younger people want what their parents have, so often they turn to a doldrum, compounded interest type routine that definitely includes booze, because the billboard says 'Rocky Mountain Man.' But that is unrewarding. There is no man from the Rockies. Younger kids are by default more accepting of ideas and concepts, but also more fierce in rejections of ideas and concepts. A real Yin and Yang. The pendulum swings pretty radically and frequently. It is an age of wisdom gathering and many things are new and shiny. It is when that shiny starts to wear off. From there, who knows what happens. Maybe they spark, ignite and change. Maybe they fall into the routine of the matrix type socio sycophantic miming of what the Jones's are doing? Or maybe they are smart enough to realize some intellectual nuggets and become the 1% - the Irish Mafia member that breaks one of the shackles of life off of their existence - booze and substances. Moving on.

Be honest with yourself, find a catalyst and begin your artful transformation to be sober. Being honest with yourself should also begin with knowing who you are. We want you to roll the dice on yourself and win by carrying your own weight. Your own social ontology position.

Identify your being as a tool to help form you as the person overcoming the abuse. You can also choose to bounce these traits off of people in an honest fashion to reveal truths you didn't know existed. While this is fun, it may also be brutally nihilistic and eye opening, but provide some breakthroughs for you personally, and possibly professionally. Try to look at yourself as another person. Be honest and embrace it. This is going all in on yourself, your own name, and your own abilities. Bet on you!

Now let's get down to serious business.

Step 1: Identify Yourself - The Four Seasons

Describing human personalities in the context of the four seasons is an intriguing way to explore how individuals may exhibit different traits, behaviors, and preferences. Each season carries its own unique characteristics, rhythms, and moods, which can correlate to how people feel and behave. In this exploration, we will delve into how human personalities might align with the qualities of spring, summer, autumn, and winter. Notably, these traits appear across all ages and can be observed even in children as young as five or six. There are, of course, outliers, but most people tend to exhibit one dominant seasonal trait blended with a secondary one. It is not usually 50/50, but definitely a blend.

Spring

Spring personalities are often associated with renewal, growth, and optimism. Much like the season itself, individuals with a spring personality tend to be energetic, enthusiastic, and chock full of potential. They may possess a youthful exuberance and an eagerness to explore new opportunities. Spring personalities are often colorful, creative and adaptable, embracing change and transformation with a sense of excitement. They may be natural leaders, inspiring others with their vision and passion. At their best, spring personalities are vibrant, resilient, and constantly evolving. They dress in pastels and bright colors, don't really worry about the price of gasoline, sort of know what is in their bank account, like to bake and throw smaller parties, and drink white wines. Jewelry is playful and whimsical, matching their outfits, though usually not expensive if purchased by themselves, but they will spend a bit on it as a gift for someone they care about. Prices on a restaurant menu matter to a degree. They are willing to pay more for higher quality, but view it as a treat, since they are typically making dinners at home. However, they may also struggle with impatience or inconsistency, as they can sometimes be prone to jumping from one idea to the next without fully following through.

Summer

Summer personalities radiate warmth, vitality, and sociability. Like the long, sun-drenched days of summer, individuals with a summer personality are often outgoing, charismatic, and magnetic. They love a good party, spontaneous or planned, on the beach, a boat, or the backyard. Use of alcohol amplifies these feelings. They thrive in social settings, effortlessly connecting on some surface level with others and spreading joy wherever they go. They love hearing your story and then telling their story. They wear what the season calls for. Flip flops at the beach, choose sneakers to the gym, dress shoes for dinner, and who knows what to the mud volleyball games. Jewelry is an accessory and they don't spend much on it, but do appreciate it if gifted. Summer personalities are typically confident and ambitious, with a natural ability to seize opportunities and make things happen. Usually this type of person is the one convincing others the activity will be fun. They may possess a strong sense of purpose and determination, pursuing their goals with unwavering focus and drive. At their best, summer personalities are generous, inspiring, and capable of achieving great success. Prices on a menu are somewhat irrelevant, as they assume someone else is picking up the tab, or it will be split, often favoring their menu decision. If they are paying, they order frugally. They definitely do not know or care about the price of gas, as they are not the ones usually paying. If the dog collar is cute, they buy it. However, they may also struggle with burnout or a fear of missing out, as they can sometimes overextend themselves in their pursuit of excitement and stimulation.

Autumn

Autumn personalities are characterized by depth, introspection, and wisdom. Much like the changing colors of the leaves, individuals with an autumn personality have a rich inner world and a keen insight into the complexities of life. They may be thoughtful, analytical, and contemplative, seeking to understand the deeper meaning behind their experiences and relationships. They analyze their social ontology and make tweaks to it based on a return on their time. Autumn personalities are often introspective, valuing solitude and self-reflection as opportunities for personal growth and development. They may possess a quiet strength and resilience, navigating life's challenges with grace and wisdom. This introspection is often paired, sometimes unhelpfully, with alcohol as a coping mechanism. Price of gas? They are the ones that will drive 11 miles to save 7¢ a gallon. They don't want to pull money out of a high fee ATM, so they adjust accordingly. These types may clip coupons, and definitely look for a deal. These types play the credit card air miles game at great cost to their time. Jewelry is only worn as a necessity, if at all. A watch tells time, not their personality (intentionally). Prices on a menu are relevant, and their dining out decisions are primarily based on the value the menu provides. They like happy hour deals and will sacrifice a decision based on cost. At their best, autumn personalities are wise, empathetic, and deeply attuned to the needs of others. Think of engineers, lawyers, and other detailed oriented professions as folks that fit this profile. However, they may also struggle with indecision or melancholy, as they can sometimes become lost in their own thoughts and emotions.

Winter

Winter personalities are marked by introspection and resilience. Like the quiet stillness of a snowy landscape, individuals with a winter personality are often calm, composed, and contemplative. They may possess a quiet strength and resilience, weathering life's storms with grace and poise. Winter personalities value solitude and self-reflection as opportunities for personal growth and development. The price of gas is irrelevant, they have to get from A to B regardless of the price. Time is money. They will go to an ATM and if the fees are high, they will pull out more money to drop the percentage of the fee as a total of the transaction. Prices on menus are of no concern, as they are dining for a purpose other than eating. This personality type will ruin a good pair of shoes to get a job done if required, as they know the job at hand is most likely providing a high return on time invested. They wear a winter vest too long into Spring and too early in the fall, as it is a versatile piece of clothing that can easily be removed. It is not part of their outfit, but rather a tool. They may be deeply philosophical, seeking to understand the deeper meaning behind their experiences and relationships. Winter personalities are often characterized by their patience, perseverance, and stoicism, facing challenges with a sense of inner strength and resolve. These types come across as brash sometimes, when in reality, they already know their answer and do not want to waste valuable time moving forward on a fool's errand. At their best, winter personalities are wise, resilient, and deeply grounded. However, they may also struggle with feelings of isolation or detachment, using alcohol frequently, as they can sometimes become overly withdrawn or distant from others.

Overall, while each season offers its own unique qualities and characteristics, human personalities are complex and multifaceted, and individuals exhibit traits from multiple seasons depending on the context and circumstances of their lives. By understanding how each seasonal quality manifests in behavior, we can gain insight into our own tendencies around alcohol. This in turn will help to foster deeper connections and appreciation for the richness of the human experience in our sober journey and social ontology. You may now realize your Aunt was not being a bitch but coming from a place of genuine care regarding your excessive over the top behavior one day in the past. You didn't know her 'personality type' because you were so narrowly focused on yourself. Now you can employ this new information to intercept information about your world and theirs a bit differently. Assess yourself and slowly begin to assess others that are helping you along your journey. This is a powerful tool. We have included a check box exercise to help you get started on this area of your journey.

Self-Assessment: Identifying Your Seasonal Personality

Check all statements that feel true *most of the time*. There are no right or wrong answers.

Spring

☐ I feel energized by new ideas and fresh starts
☐ I enjoy planning small gatherings or creative projects
☐ I'm optimistic and tend to focus on potential rather than limits
☐ I'm more spontaneous than structured
☐ I value experiences over strict budgets

Summer

☐ I thrive in social settings and enjoy being around people
☐ I'm often the one encouraging others to join in or have fun
☐ I enjoy attention, storytelling, and shared experiences
☐ I'm comfortable taking risks or "going with the flow"
☐ I don't stress much about costs in the moment

Autumn

☐ I think deeply before making decisions
☐ I value efficiency, practicality, and return on time or money
☐ I'm comfortable spending time alone
☐ I often analyze situations before acting
☐ I'm cautious with spending and prefer good value

Winter

☐ I'm highly independent and goal-focused
☐ I prioritize outcomes over appearances
☐ I'm comfortable making unpopular but practical decisions
☐ I value time more than money
☐ I tend to withdraw when focused on a task or problem

Scoring & Reflection

- The season with the **most checked boxes** is likely your **primary personality type**
- The season with the **second-most checks** is likely your **secondary influence**
- Most people are **not** evenly split—and that's normal

Reflection Questions

- How does alcohol typically show up in my dominant season?
- Does drinking amplify my strengths—or my blind spots?
- What seasonal traits might I want to lean into *without* alcohol?

Awareness comes before change. This exercise isn't about labeling—it's about noticing patterns.

2. The Challenge: Your Plan of Attack

Visualization

The absolute best athletes in the world are coached in a way that naturally breeds winning. You are no different. You just don't have a dedicated coach showing up to practice with you every day for seven to ten hours. You may need a 'coach' to bump you along or you may not. We believe you only need a mirror and one powerful tool used by top performers everywhere: visualization. We will teach you this tool.

If you are not familiar with how professional athletes train, it is intense. More intense than you can imagine. They practice on the field of play, no matter the heat or cold. The training is video recorded. Coaches review hours of footage, noting what works, what needs refinement, and what must change. The player is not offended; the player wants to get better. The player then visualizes the next practice and what key functions will be tweaked to make their performance better. From there, the efforts to fine tune begin, repeat, and never stop. The coaches and players also integrate contingencies, mishaps, and other out of pocket experiences that a person may not expect, but could certainly happen. Weather, new opposing team or teammates unexpectedly switched out, their diet, and more. The player continually visualizes the play over and over and over. If sports don't resonate with you, consider actors. Same thing. They practice their lines over and over until the actor and director agree on the perfect delivery. The examples go on. We are interested in visualization here, not the profession.

When it comes to alcohol, total avoidance may be the ultimate goal, but first, you need realistic, visualized milestones. You can replay the proverbial tape of past experiences to see how alcohol shaped the outcome. As you embark on this visualization effort, reiterate to yourself this mantra: You are not depriving yourself by choosing not to drink; you are investing in immediate and future value. Stop making situations more difficult than they are by thinking they shouldn't be difficult in the first place. You will begin to act on conviction, back your own instincts, and take ownership of your future. From a business perspective, you are self-funding your growth.

How to visualize

If you want to get nerdy, the visualization process we are about to embark upon is defined by professionals as katathym-imaginative psychotherapy.

> *It is a mind-body intervention by which a trained practitioner or teacher helps a participant or patient to evoke and generate mental images that simulate or recreate the sensory perception of sights, sounds, tastes, smells, movements, and images associated with touch, such as texture, temperature, and pressure, as well as imaginative or mental content that the participant or patient experiences as defying conventional sensory categories, and that may precipitate strong emotions or feelings in the absence of the stimuli (alcohol in this case) to which correlating sensory receptors are receptive.*

This process is what psychologists call katathym-imaginative psychotherapy—a method that uses vivid mental imagery to simulate real experiences and emotional responses. That's putting it succinctly. In the case of moving your martini, you are trying it out as a self-guided psychotherapy. If you would like professional help in this arena, we are sure there are folks qualified in your area to do so.

In order to achieve something great in real life, you must first achieve it in your mind. You have to create a mental picture before you manifest it in real life. Visualization is simply the act of repeating a series of events in your mind that you want to achieve in real life. A degree of internal obsession is acceptable. You will drive your friends bonkers if you bring up your visualizations to them every chance you get. It is healthy to discuss these ideas with the right audience. Now let's begin to own your shot.

Your mental training should include both positive and negative possibilities. Planning for the worst is hard, but needs to be visualized. That prepares you for all eventualities. Life isn't always a winning lottery ticket. You're most likely not going to make a video library of every possible event that could occur if you do or do not drink, but you can most likely find pictures on your phone of you after you have had a few drinks or whatnot. That is a good start of where you no longer want to be.

Now find those pictures of you sober. Compare the two sets. Imagine how the moment in time would have been different in the first picture, had you not been drinking. Would you have been better off? Would you have even been there? Would you have gotten into that drunken fight with your brother about how you are raising your 3 year old? Who knows, but visualize it.

Planning for the worst in a sober state of mind reduces panic. You begin to not worry about anything. You become more in control. You are generating a blueprint for every possibility, whether it's good or bad. This blueprint is very important. How can you start becoming sober with visualization?

First things first, you need to learn how to relax your body & come into a calm state.

What are the criteria for mastering visualization?

1. It should be vivid
2. You should rehearse every possibility many times
3. Experience it like it is already happening to you in the present
You've already chosen not to drink hundreds, if not thousands of times in your visualization.

Everybody has heard about routines. Some even follow a physical routine. We rely heavily on meeting the challenge of a solid, consistent mental routine that works for you. Instead of looking at nonsense on your phone at night, look at current pictures of you enjoying sobriety at night before you sleep. Develop a routine that generates positive feelings. In our example, these pictures are clips of every successful possibility to the challenge of becoming consistently sober and staying sober. These pictures are you investing in yourself.

Visualize every moment from your starting in the morning on top of your bed, through each AM ritual, into the day, the afternoon, and then at night, until you emerge from the success of the day's outcome to go to bed once again, victorious in your efforts to be sober. Visualize this success.

It's a choice of how quickly and deeply you want to do your visualization. You can insert scenarios, possibilities, interactions, conversations, activities, whatever you desire. Just visualize the experience like it has happened 10, 100, or 1,000 times. If and when it does happen, it most likely will not happen exactly as you visualized, but it will be so close to an emulation that you will handle it beautifully and be confident you could do it again. You should notice that a 'visualized' experience may become a building block, or not, and you can decide what to do further with it. The real catch here is repetition, creating involuntary imagery into voluntary imagery. You have to practice it daily, not just occasionally. You have to ingrain every scene in your subconscious. So in a real scenario, your subconscious can overtake your conscious. Bruce Lee says he fears a person that has practiced one kick 10,000 times but thinks a fool of a person who practices 10,000 kicks 1 time. That is visualization in practice.

Always remember that things work smoothly when it's controlled by the subconscious. Last but not least, master how to set goals and achieve them. Setting goals also has a critical element many forget - the Why. What purpose is your goal of sobriety without a reason?

To master a set of goals, you need your WHY in your pocket at all times. Not just the simple WHY, but the deep rooted, foundational reason that you build off of that is leading to a paradigm shift in the way you think. The interesting thing here is that this particular Irish Mafia method of visualization coupled with your WHY can be utilized in many aspects of your life, not just as it relates to being sober. It becomes your new set of instincts to live by. Let it live rent free in your mind and produce additional outcomes for many other aspects of your life.

Paradigm Shift:
A radical change in thinking from an accepted point of view to a new belief.

At this point, you can also determine if you would like to adopt the gradual change or the sudden change. If you are slowly reducing your drinking, you are in the 'gradual' camp. If you 'quit cold turkey', you are in the 'sudden' camp. To quit drinking, The Art of Sober thinks you need to be focused on one or the other, and that depends on your resolve. Now let's get to the why's of your goals. Moving your martini is applying this tried and true technique to get to your 'why' for almost any alcohol related situation.

The Five Whys: Getting to the Answer

The practice of asking "why" five times—often called the Five Whys—is a powerful, business-minded problem-solving method designed to uncover root causes.

In practice, you ask "why" repeatedly; by the fifth time, you should arrive at a genuine answer. Struggle is where your rebirth begins. At The Art of Sober, we view the first "why" as the beginning of recovery. This struggle should eventually feel natural as a necessary and positive part of growth. The struggle leads to contemplation and growth. Be creative, authentic, assertive, and honest in coming up with your questions. Take your time. Craft your why, review it, make adjustments, and eventually settle on it and move forward. This section is central to your journey. While it may feel repetitive at times, each thread contributes to the larger fabric of sobriety.

Below are several key benefits of using the Five Whys in sobriety.

Identifying the Root Cause

By asking "Why?" repeatedly, you delve deeper into the underlying factors contributing to a problem. This helps you move beyond surface-level symptoms to identify the fundamental cause of the issue.

As an exercise, start with asking 'why do I drink' just to get the proverbial ball rolling and your brain into gear. You may reach clarity by the third or fourth "why."

Basic reasons for drinking stem from various factors, and the reasons can vary greatly from person to person. No shit. But let's get a little deeper.

To help you along, here are some very common reasons why people may drink excessively:

Social Pressure

Peer pressure or social norms may influence individuals to drink more than they originally intended, especially in social settings where alcohol consumption is common and encouraged. Sports games, after work happy hours, graduation parties, etc. You certainly do NOT have to drink, but if everyone around you is grabbing a beer from the cooler, a person will most likely just put one out in front of you. Having a non-alcoholic drink of some sort in your hand already occupying that sacred real estate and voilà, the moment passes.

Stress Relief

Many people turn to alcohol as a way to cope with stress, anxiety, or other negative emotions. After an argument, you grab a drink to cool off. Tough day at work, same. Fender bender, drink. Had to take the garbage to the curb? Drink. Alcohol's sedative effects can provide temporary relief from emotional distress, leading some individuals to use it as a form of self-medication.

Escapism

Alcohol seems to offer an escape from reality or difficult situations. Some individuals may drink excessively to avoid facing personal problems, relationship issues, or other challenges in their lives. Declaring bankruptcy is a major problem that could most certainly lead someone to drink to forget. Getting dumped by a girlfriend, possible. Look beneath the surface and look at a problem that pushed you to crack a bottle. As we move our martini, if you think you have a problem, go find a bigger one.

Boredom or Loneliness

Feelings of boredom or loneliness can drive people to drink excessively in an attempt to alleviate feelings of emptiness or boredom and seek social connection or stimulation. This happens more frequently than people think. Watching TV and cracking a bottle is an easy move. Three drinks later, you're likely no longer following the show. We are not judging, just pointing it out. Ask WHY you drink when bored, if it happens frequently.

Genetic Predisposition

Some individuals may have a genetic predisposition to alcoholism or addictive behaviors, making them more susceptible to developing problematic drinking patterns. The jury is out on this reason, but it cannot be discounted. Bodies wire and rewire over time. Humans have been around for a long time. So as science has genetically sliced plants to derive a 'better plant' your ancestry has been genetically altering itself for centuries. If you believe this is a main reason for your drinking, you may want to consult a professional to explore this. Alas, we try to avoid crutches and 'shoulder shrugs' when we can. Believing it's genetic is not a free pass to this behavior. It may make it more difficult to reduce or stop altogether your habits, but it is not an obstacle you cannot overcome. I drink because I am Irish. Loser. I'm hairy because I am Italian. Most likely.

Trauma or Past Experiences

Traumatic experiences or unresolved emotional issues from the past can contribute to excessive drinking as individuals may use alcohol as a way to numb emotional pain or cope with traumatic memories. Visualize these memories to move from involuntary to voluntary cognizance. Basically, something happened to you and you were mentally unable to comprehend what was happening. It is now time to address those experiences and sort out in a reasonable fashion what happened. Growing up with an absolute shit haircut, where bangs were cut along the taped line because the family was on welfare is not enough trauma to drink. Alas finding the root cause of the actual 'traumatic experience' doesn't' change the fact that the incident occurred, but somehow will magically, and if you have a sense of humor, sometimes make it less traumatic - in retrospect of course. There are countless books on past trauma emotional issues and how it affects the 'current' or future you. We could go on forever. If this is an area of intense personal pain, definitely reach out for more books or professional help on your childhood trauma. Getting duct taped to a tree in your underwear, facing the front door of a hot girls house, and your brother rings the doorbell, then ditches? That was fun. At least she helped me get untangled!

If you are into Pity Parties, dwelling on past experiences is right up your alley. It allows a person to basically lay blame for how 'fucked up' they might be or justify some behaviors, especially while drinking. You should work hard on this area if it affects you greatly.

Dwelling exclusively on the past often becomes a justification rather than a solution.

Newsflash, the judge presiding over your DUI case is not going to provide leniency upon hearing your defense attorney say,

"Well, Hizzoner, while climbing his favorite pine tree in 4th grade with some friends, my client's brother was on top of the tree and peed on my client - his OWN brother. Raining urine everywhere, my client and all 6 of his friends basically jumped out of the tree, falling 8 feet to the ground, hitting branches on the way down, but miraculously survived. Alas, he is still traumatized to this day at 37 years old from the great Tree Pee incident. His past trauma caused him to recently drink and drive, so can we cut him a break and give him probation and reduce the fines by 50%?"

Not happening. Past trauma will not excuse present-day consequences. Courts—and life—don't work that way.

If you're blaming past experiences for your drinking, we suggest the following:

1) STOP living in the past. It is a highway littered with choices, and some of them were bad. Focus on the good ones, file them in your brain, and start visualizing your future.

2) NO ONE really wants to hear about the past. As Tony Soprano says, the conversations that start with 'remember when' are the absolute lowest form of conversation. It is about not dwelling on the past, but rather understanding that things change in life. If you are reminded of who you *were*, it can trap you there. Possible past bad or destructive decisions, repackaged as legendary, subtly romanticize habits you are trying to outgrow. Start your legacy now, today, immediately.

3) Deal professionally with your past experiences, but do not let it anchor you down from gaining new growth and moving forward in life. That said, nostalgia isn't the enemy. It becomes a problem when it replaces present connection, glorifies self-sabotage, or prevents identity evolution. Healthy growth sounds more like, "Look how far we've come," instead of, "Remember how wild we used to be?" Learn from the past as an experience.

Environmental Factors

Environmental factors such as easy access to alcohol, cultural attitudes toward drinking, and advertising and marketing of alcohol products can influence drinking behavior. Consumerism at its finest. Not one of the 'hot people' in the ads would ever talk to you. If advertising reflected reality after three or four hours of drinking, consumption would plummet. Notice how some beer commercials focus on Clydesdales only? They push an emotional connection to a larger identity. Why? Because they think you are stupid.

Almost every major sporting event around the world encourages alcohol. A famous billboard that certainly didn't win any awards just simply stated "Liquid Fun" next to a picture of a beer can. That's the message. Ads clearly state a benefit. We could go on for days about the marketing ecosystem of alcohol. It is in your face. Most of the time they don't even try to make it sexy, fun, adventuresome or life changing. They just put a lazy tagline on it and know most will drink anyways.

May we suggest a simple observational exercise whereby you take 1 'normal day' in your routine and try to tick mark every time you see messaging for alcohol. Please also include the number of stores it is available at as you travel around in your routine. It is a massively big business of selling, and conversely, of people dying, but they don't want the dying from alcohol messages out there. Your mind will be blown by the conscientious tabulation of alcohol messaging. Cigarettes can no longer be advertised in many mediums, why not alcohol? We always say, follow the money.

Mental Health Disorders

Co-occurring mental health disorders such as depression, bipolar disorder, or post-traumatic stress disorder (PTSD) can increase the risk of excessive drinking as individuals may use alcohol as a form of self-medication to alleviate symptoms. This is about as serious as it gets. It is very difficult to 'hold in mind' some imagery, as it can certainly redirect away from the specific cognitive task of being sober. In other words, it is very powerful to overcome. We suggest strong clinical support in this case. Sure we pepper humor in this book, but if you have clinical issues diagnosed, and your current doctor is not responding to your needs, consult another doctor. Your life matters and the sooner you get onto the path to meaningful recovery, the better. We are not medical professionals, but encourage you to seek one out.

If you believe you suffer from this as a main reason to drink, we strongly suggest consulting a professional to redirect your approach to drinking. It's all fun and games, until it's not.

Family History

Growing up in an environment where excessive drinking is normalized or having family members with a history of alcoholism can increase the likelihood of developing problematic drinking habits. No shit. This is a common reason why a lot of folks drink.

Person A, "Why do you drink?"

You, "Not 100% sure but I've been around it all my life. Never thought about it, really."

That is a common exchange. Alas, we say break the mold. You can point to the past, but now is time to take control. Go all in on yourself. There is a reason some of the fastest cars in the world do not have a rearview mirror. When you are moving forward, you don't care what is behind you. Reframe your thinking, stop dwelling on the past history, and lay claim to the newfound you. Do not be anchored in your past glorified dysfunction. There is uncharted territory to be conquered. Be proud that you are making this change. It will most likely not be easy, but brick by brick, you are building a new house to proverbially live in.

It's interesting, many families cling on to the 'first kid to go to a 4 year college' in their family, but won't celebrate as quickly about the first kid to be sober. Flip your script and become the strong family member that leads by example. It will no doubt become a talking point of sorts for a few moments, then everyone goes back to their daily grind. What might happen is that a few members decide to follow your sober lead. Whether you are a natural born leader, or a sheep that cannot lift your own fork up to eat, waiting for your Mummy to do it, by deciding not to drink, you just stepped over a threshold very few do. You can do it.

Let the family say what they want, and realize you have to live your life, not theirs. If this means detaching from your family, that is a completely separate topic, but a concept worth exploring in order to achieve the goals you have set for yourself, no matter the timeline of the goals. Sometimes it is necessary to sever relationships, even close family ones. Growth requires space, sometimes a lot of space. As a famous person says, 'there are meetings and partings.' You may tend to find that if you are the first mover with a set of balls (or ovaries), others will follow. Your sobriety or reduced drinking will most likely be encouraging news. They may not declare it anywhere, but when you see them next, they might express the fact that they reduced or quit drinking because of you. No one person honestly has the full grasp of the impact they have on people. Be confident that even though you do not have a direct feedback loop, people are watching. Of course, this might hurt if you relapse for a day or a week or so if you are 100% sober. It would be natural to think you are letting not only yourself down, but them as well. It can happen. They are watching. We suggest you shut out that feedback loop if necessary and achieve your goals for you, not for them. Your commitment to sobriety must come first. Do not dwell on a relapse, get back in the trenches. Look how far you have gotten and keep your momentum.

Next we present a simple worksheet for the Five Whys in order to get to the root cause of drinking.

Worksheet: The Five Whys (Getting to the Real Answer)

Purpose:

This exercise helps you move beyond surface explanations and uncover the *true* reason behind your drinking. Take your time. Write honestly. No one else needs to see this.

Struggle is not failure, it's where clarity begins.

Step 1: Start with the Question

Primary Question:
Why do I drink?

Write your first, most immediate answer. Don't overthink it.

Why #1:

____

____

____

Step 2: Ask "Why?" Again
Now ask why your first answer is true.
Why #2:

—

Step 3: Go Deeper

This is often where discomfort begins. Stay with it.

Why #3:

____

____

____

Step 4: The Turning Point

Answers here often shift from habits to beliefs or emotions.

Why #4:

____

____

____

Step 5: The Root

This answer should feel **quiet**, **clear**, and **undeniable**.
If it feels defensive, go back one step.

Why #5:

____

____

____

Reflection Check

Read your five answers from top to bottom.

☐ Do my answers move from *behavior* to *belief?*
☐ Do they become more specific rather than vague?
☐ Does the final answer feel true—even if I don't like it?

If not, revisit **Why #3 or #4** and continue.

Your Catalyst (One Sentence Only)

Now distill everything into **one clear sentence**.

My reason for changing my relationship with alcohol is:

____

____

(If this takes more than one sentence, it isn't ready yet.)

Reality Test

Ask yourself:

- Would I still choose this reason on a hard day? ☐Yes ☐No
- Does this reason belong to *me*, not someone else? ☐Yes ☐No
- Does this reason move me forward? ☐Yes ☐No

If you checked **No** anywhere, revise your catalyst.

Important Notes

- Your answer may change over time—and that's healthy.
- This is not a one-time exercise. Revisit it every few months.
- Your "why" is a **tool**, not a slogan.

Clarity beats motivation. Every time.

The Five Whys Lead to Worthwhile Change

Understanding the root cause allows you to create solutions that address the problem directly and prevent it from recurring. This work requires grit, perseverance, and mindfulness, but it can be done.

"Recurring drinking" typically refers to a pattern of regular or repeated alcohol consumption over time. It varies in frequency, duration, and quantity. This depends on personal habits and situations. Whether you drink a full bottle of wine every night or only one glass on weekends, the pattern is still recurring. Let's try to break that habitual pattern. Some would argue that even only drinking on Sunday night your 1 glass of wine is an 'alcoholic' by definition. Reflect on your personal goals and do not worry about those chumps putting a label on things. Pointing a finger at someone leaves that person with three fingers pointing back at themselves. March forward with your progress. Work on one habit, slowly, at a time. Do not care what other people think about you.

Recurring drinking patterns vary from moderate to heavy. Moderate drinking is up to one drink a day for women and two for men. Heavy drinking means exceeding these limits regularly. That is the textbook definition of recurring drinking patterns. Don't fool yourself into pretending this is normal. Be honest about how much you drink, what you drink, when you drink, and, most importantly, why you drink.

Recurring drinking can become a problem. This often happens when it leads to issues like poor judgment, health problems, or relationship troubles. Legal issues and trouble with daily life can also arise. Plus, hangovers can take away your health and time.

Take a moment to write down what you could gain by cutting back or skipping drinks during your usual routine. Fewer mistakes while cooking dinner for the kids? Less time zoning out in front of the TV? Less of what and more of what. We will get into journaling more later, but as a discipline, think about it.

Some people turn to alcohol to cope with life's challenges. There may be more than one reason behind the action. A narrow mind credits drinking to solve some common issues. Let's look at those and try to break from the "I'm only doing it because" mindset as you reduce your alcohol consumption. Further, in general , this mindset leads to a miserable existence, even if you are stone cold sober. "I only do it because" is a dangerous place to be. You might not have discovered your universal purpose yet, but you act because you are human, not a robot. Your internal dialogue can assist you in this.

Here are some common issues people think alcohol can fix. If one stands out, please note it.

Stress Relief

Alcohol's sedative effects can provide temporary relief from stress, anxiety, or tension. Some people see alcohol as a way to relax after a long day. They might use it to deal with work stress or personal issues. Typically this is very temporary. The cold reality of you getting shit canned from your job isn't going away because you cracked open a shitty beer. Meditate, take a walk, watch birds on a tree. Get grounded. Touch grass - literally. It is important to learn alternative, and more meaningful, coping mechanisms. It probably won't be as easy as cracking a beer to start. Still, it can lead to breakthroughs in managing the stressful situation step by step. Research some basic breathing exercises as well. That will come in handy.

Emotional Pain

Alcohol can numb emotional pain or distress for a limited time. Some people use alcohol to feel better. It helps them cope with sadness, loneliness, grief, or trauma. There's that pesky word 'trauma' again. Did you lose an arm? No? Good. Let's move on. We can't define trauma for you. It's personal. We suggest talking to a professional to explore your thoughts on what trauma means to you. We say, if you think you have a problem, go find a bigger one.

Just so you know where The Art of Sober is coming from, as a baseline, Vietnam teenage wasteland and Iraq war type frontline battlefields count as trauma in our opinion. A person who called you fat in 6th grade does not. There is a difference, in our opinion, on real, life altering trauma vs mental hurt and kids being dopey kids. Again, we cannot stress enough, consult a professional if your mental state of mind is concerning you or a loved one. Now, should you down 4 cans of beer because your Mom said you looked like you were getting fat? Yes and no. Yes, if you are still a drinker and weak minded and have no intentions of quitting, etc. No, if you are artful in your sobriety. You elevate yourself and come to the realization that your Mom knows no difference and cannot help herself in the 'commenting on your life' dept. You're mature. You don't let the compression of the interaction affect you. You laugh and shrug it off as part of her nature and love for you. If she really loved you, she might have bore knowledge on how to lead a healthier lifestyle and not go through the fast food drive through every chance she had when she was raising you. But we digress, that is a past trauma and we collectively don't give a shit about that. Your Mom did the best she could at the time with what she had at the time. Move on to your bigger problems.

Social Anxiety - A Big Trigger

Alcohol can lower inhibitions and ease social anxiety. This makes it easier for some people to socialize and feel more comfortable in social situations. We are going to delve deep into how to handle anxiety.

What is hilarious about this paradox is a lot of folks are scared to act like imbeciles in front of people, thus the anxiety. Yet, 2 shots of tequila in, they lower their inhibitions and act like complete morons. Alcohol can make you less aware of your surroundings. This creates a false sense of reality. It can truly dupe you into thinking what you are doing is 'part of the liquid fun' and encourages you to increase said behaviors. No one thinks 4 shirtless fat dudes sitting around a fire at a family campsite at 10pm, yelling nonsensical words is cool, except those 4 dudes. There is also the flip side, whereby 'executive minded persons' that would never be caught dead sitting with our 4 campfire dudes are drinking to fit in, just in a different manner. They want to badly be accepted by the crowd they are canoodling with. They choose their drink carefully, use longer syllable words, and flaunt goofy ass 'leisure shoes' while wearing a suit - makes no sense to the shirtless dudes, but to each their own. Each person in each group is trying to fit into their tribe, their social ontological group, at some level. Some are situated, some are new, some are lost and haven't realized it yet. The common glue—the unifying force—is alcohol. In a social setting that makes you anxious, you might avoid talking to someone. But then, you grab a bottle, and suddenly, the issue feels 'solved.'

We offer a few critical, yet basic, easy to adopt methods to overcome social anxiety besides drinking. In fact, the heaviest hitting way to overcome anxiety is to NOT be drinking. Sure, you might think you are standing out like a sore thumb, but the truth is, no one really gives a fuck about your decision, and you should not give a fuck about them. Do they pay your bills? Are they raising your kids? Are they really that important? No. Give a fuck about yourself FIRST.

Prepare Ahead of Time

Before attending a function, mentally prepare yourself by setting realistic expectations. Remind yourself that it's okay to feel nervous and that you don't need to be perfect. Prepare a few conversation starters; movies, books, travel, pets, or local events and avoid politics or religion. Pick a current event, hobby or something you know a bit about. The latest TV shows or pets are always a winner. Maybe compliment someone on their choice of jewelry. Pro tip - edification. Talk about other folks very positively in an authentic manner and you will find others relax around you, making the entire shindig even more pleasant.

Arrive Early

Getting to the event early can help you settle in before it gets busy. This allows you to gradually acclimate to the setting and have more one-on-one interactions before larger groups form. This helps on many levels most people cannot comprehend. It takes time, energy and effort to prepare, plan and put on a function, no matter the size. Get there early, about 20 minutes max. Ask the host if they need help, and just assess the situation. By contributing, you are gaining a slight advantage over the other guests in that you can stay out of the way, or be helpful, to the hosts. If you're not drinking, ask for your favorite drink early. This way, you can skip that talk while everyone is around. It helps you avoid curious eyes and ears. If you brought your own cooler or whatnot, position it early and you are good to go.

Focus on Others

Instead of dwelling on your own anxiety, shift your focus onto other people at the event. Ask them open-ended questions about themselves and listen attentively to their responses. This can help take the pressure off yourself and make interactions feel more natural. Find the person staring at the TV by themselves or on their phones in a corner and start a conversation. No doubt you are not the only person feeling awkward at the party. If you have a companion, tag team other singletons and bring them into the fold, they will appreciate it. Edify folks when the time is right, especially the hosts and the effort they put into the event. This skill may come naturally. If not, hone it over time. You know your seasonal personality type, play a game and guess other personalities.

Take Breaks When Needed

It's okay to take breaks from socializing if you start to feel overwhelmed. Excuse yourself to get some fresh air, use the restroom, or take a short walk outside. Taking breaks can help you recharge and regroup before rejoining any event. Leaving early is also 100% acceptable. Classic Irish Goodbye comes in handy a lot.

Practice Relaxation Techniques

If you start to feel anxious, practice your relaxation techniques such as deep breathing or mindfulness meditation. Focus on your breath and try to let go of any tension or negative thoughts. These techniques can help calm your mind and reduce physical symptoms of anxiety. While you are at the function 'alone' you are not alone. There are many folks around you that may be feeling the same way, or worse. Avoid petty comments that may come across as misconstrued. Comment on how 'great' something is like a piece of art on the wall, or how great their pet is. Don't relax by closing your eyes and humming loud, they'll think you got possessed! Got tourettes? Maybe avoid small parties.

Set Realistic Goals

Set small, achievable goals at the party instead of trying to engage with everyone. Try having a good chat with one or two people. You can also join a group activity. Celebrate your accomplishments, no matter how small they may seem. This is mission critical.

Choose two topics:

- One that's new to you. This will help you connect with someone who has strong opinions and learn from them.
- Another that you're very familiar with. This way, you can share your insights confidently.

Reward Yourself

After the party, reward yourself for facing your social anxiety and attending the event. Enjoy something nice. Watch your favorite movie, take a relaxing bath, or spend time with a loved one. Recognize and acknowledge your efforts, regardless of the outcome of the party. Small steps lead to great success. Again, Rome wasn't built in a day and the first bread recipe wasn't Focaccia.

Remember that overcoming social anxiety takes time and practice. Be patient with yourself and celebrate your improved progress along the way. If social anxiety affects your daily life, think about getting help from a mental health professional. They can offer support and treatment options. Do not let booze help you cope.

Additional Issues People Believe Alcohol Can Solve
Escape from Reality

Some people use alcohol to escape their problems. It helps them forget their responsibilities or tough situations, at least for a while. The hard truth is that escapism is temporary. A reprieve may feel good, but it doesn't last long. This impermanence is part of alcohol's addictive pull. It's like going to the House of Mirrors at the amusement park and seeing yourself in various mirrors. In some mirrors you look great, some mirrors you look goofy in, and all of them are a 100% departure from reality. Alcohol is no different. Once you walk out of the House of Mirrors,—boom—you're back to yourself and your reality. Not the distorted reality.

The odd thing most people may not internalize is that the House of Mirrors is 100% awful. The easily amused love it. If you're reading this book, you're likely past being easily amused. The House of Mirrors is a tricky place. It twists how we see things and bends light in interesting ways. You look grotesque in one mirror, then svelte and dashing in another. In the next, you appear as a fat turd, then skinny as a pencil. Sometimes, you look like a lovely midget. It keeps changing. The House of Mirrors takes you on a journey through your essence. It doesn't change you physically, but it does shift your mindset. People that are easily amused just walk out and move on to the next muse - the next thing that makes them feel excited or curious.

People who are self-aware may leave the House of Mirrors flooded with "what if" questions. If they're careful, they consider those 'what if' scenarios. They know they won't become a midget or pencil-thin. But what if that did happen? Insert Kafka references here. This sharp self-awareness helps you break through. It empowers your choice not to drink. Instead of staying trapped in "what if," you begin asking "how does."

"What if I am pencil thin?" turns into "How would my life look if I were thinner?"

"What if I didn't drink?" turns into "How would my life look if I didn't drink?"

"What if I were taller?" turns into "How would my life look if I were more assertive?"

"What if I were a midget?" turns into "Man, elevators would smell a whole lot different to me."

The House of Mirrors offers a brief escape from reality. But you can't truly leave if you keep drinking. How WOULD you look if you didn't drink? We are not suggesting merely physical looks, we are also incorporating perceptions. How would you look to your spouse, kids, friends, coworkers, strangers and more. Believe it or not, as shallow as it sounds, they already have a perception of how you look, most likely skewed by the House of Mirrors effect. You never truly know how you look through other people's eyes. Moving your martini loosens the grip of other people's perceptions. And when you stop drinking, you may notice those perceptions quietly shift.

Start breaking those mirrors one by one, at your own pace. Soon, only your true self will remain. Each mirror is typically either a peak or valley of an exaggeration of you. Let's delve into what it means to get to your true form.

For the sake of this exercise, your routine is you going through your House of Mirrors every day (24 hour cycles).

Moving your martini helps smooth out the daily 'peaks and valleys' we all face. It's like the mirrors in the House of Mirrors. Try to break one mirror each day as you move through the proverbial House of Mirrors every 24 hour cycle By "breaking mirrors," you lengthen the space between emotional distortions. You are stretching out the intervals it takes to get to the next mirror in the House of Mirrors when you travel through the same path in your next cycle. You spend less time reacting to distortion and more time grounded in reality. That is ok. The less mirrors the better.

The peak lasts longer, the 'downward trend' to the valley lasts longer, and the bottom out lasts longer. Eventually, the peak isn't as high and the valley isn't as low. You have systematically removed mirrors that do not correctly reflect you.

See your problems as mirrors you may have overlooked. Reframe them. Break that mirror right away. Then, look for a bigger mirror, or problem. You'll see that things aren't as bad as they seem. Each day is smashing a mirror or multiple mirrors, reducing any escapism from alcohol and getting to see the true you.

Mood elevation

Alcohol can create feelings of euphoria or lift your mood. Some people use it to boost their spirits or improve how they see life and their surroundings. Why is it there always seems to be that one person who calls for shots? As if drinking one beer and enjoying it isn't enough for this person. They think they are a fully aspirated 454 in a Chevelle muscle car from the 1970's and so they act like it. Loud, obnoxious, and wanting to get elevated quickly. When, in reality, they are a Yugo shitbox with a hole in the muffler, when it's said and done.

Shots do the trick and get you elevated and feeling 'fine' for the time being, but the toll it takes on everything else is to be noted. When you 'peel out' and start going fast and furious, other things suffer - the tires, wear and tear, and gas is used at a higher consumption rate. Think of your body like that and you might slow it down a bit, or avoid it altogether. If the colloquialism is 'open it up' by taking shots when you start to drink, you might want to temper it down.

Enhanced Confidence

Alcohol can lower inhibitions and change self-awareness. This may make some people feel more confident, assertive, or outgoing. It often happens in social or performance situations. This is summed up in two words: liquid courage.

There are many settings where you may give pause to the fact that alcohol lowers your inhibitions. Does it? Or is alcohol a crutch that is used because you were never taught real self-confidence? Here is the quick and dirty on the matter of self confidence, and Nike figured it out early: Just do it. Most people aren't paying attention to you. If you're genuine and not intentionally an asshole, that's enough. If the other person truly does think you are stupid, etc, well now you know. Consider them stupid, and you need to move on. Don't let someone's judgment bear weight on your efforts, as long as the effort is altruistic and not hurting anyone. Want to go up to that guy you like and start a conversation? Do you really need 3 beers and one shot of some nasty liqueur concoction to do it? We say no. Don't drink the booze, and just do it. You'll have 100% clarity and control.

Liquid courage often leads to beer goggles. Beer goggles apply to way more than just making someone appear more attractive. Beer goggles will have you looking at every situation in a more relaxed, uninhibited manner. The YouTube website has thousands of videos of folks doing the dumbest shit (no other way to put it) under the influence of beer goggles. Jump over a campfire? With beer goggles, it looks pretty easy and fun. Jump off a ledge into a pool. Same. Swerve your golf cart into the pond? Same. The list goes on and on. Beer goggles convince you that whatever you're about to do is harmless and fun. The thicker your beer goggles, we believe the more devastating the outcome will be of your actions.

Peer Pressure or Social Norms

Social pressure and cultural norms about drinking can lead people to drink. They may feel the need to fit in, belong, or meet social expectations. Alcohol is a common part of many social situations. It's nearly unavoidable. Just reach for something different. Let people come to you. They will. If a group shuns you for not drinking, you now have X-Ray vision. You will quickly realize they are not your group. There are other groups of folks you can congregate with that share your interests if that is what you are looking for.

Next time you're in a group, take a moment to observe everyone. Think about what personality season they might belong to. Don't imagine them in their underwear - that could be nasty, depending on where you are. Rather, imagine them not drinking. Assume they are not drinking. Once you start assuming everyone else is NOT drinking, and they are normal like you, things change. You are talking to a few of them and they mutter some bullshit along the lines of 'why are you not drinking?' You can simply reply, "Why are you drinking?" They won't reply. If they are a jackass, they might have a comeback. You can reply by stating that you have things to do later and need to remain focused on the end game, or you could use a similar quip. You will perfect it over time. No one is going to get into an argument over why you are not drinking. If they do carry on about you not drinking, then elevate your stance and just assert your higher level of maturity. They are the ones with the problem and will most likely realize it much too late after the incident. Your calm response to jokes and comments shows you're fully confident in cutting back or quitting alcohol. You are high voltage. You are the 1%, they are the 99%. You are not better than any other person, but in this arena, you are in control and know what is best for you. They can get shitfaced drunk or more, and if they need a ride, try to assist. The next day? That is for another time.

5 Whys: Collaboration and Better Outcomes

The 5 Whys technique is especially effective in group settings. It encourages collaboration, sharpens thinking, and leads to clearer, more creative solutions particularly when addressing behaviors like alcohol use. Asking hard questions together brings accountability and insight that are difficult to achieve alone.

Before going further, you must define alcohol abuse for yourself. Settle on your definition and move forward. Many people are indifferent to your drinking, and some may feel unsettled by your decision to change. That's irrelevant. The goal is not to be better than others, but to be better than who you were.

Redefining Abuse as Progress

Alcohol abuse is harmful. That truth matters. But recovery can be transformative when viewed as a process of growth rather than punishment.

Self-Awareness

Recovery demands honest reflection. It reveals patterns, motivations, and the deeper reasons behind drinking.

Growth and Discipline

Sobriety builds resilience, self-control, and healthier coping skills. These are tools that carry into every area of life.

Agency and Control

Quitting alcohol restores personal authority. You reclaim control instead of surrendering it to habit or circumstance.

Connection and Support

Recovery often involves meaningful connection with others who understand. Be selective. Limit social media; it tends to reward shallow engagement. Build your core first.

Stronger Relationships

Sobriety improves presence, communication, and trust, leading to healthier relationships.

Purpose and Well-Being

Recovery often reconnects people with their values and energy. Mental clarity and physical health improve, and the benefits compound over time—at any age.

Inspiration

Your progress may quietly inspire others. That reinforcement strengthens your own commitment.

Viewing alcohol abuse as a journey reframes struggle as forward motion. The challenges remain but so does the opportunity to build a healthier, more intentional life.

Next, we'll focus on strengthening your personal **Why**—so it holds when motivation fades.

Collaboration: Choosing the Right Allies

No one wants to sit around playing poker, feeling like the party is over. But the truth is, you are the 1%. You are the trailblazer who knows it's time to fold the proverbial cards in order to move onward and upward. You either keep playing along or you move on. The choice is yours.

Choose your collaborators with the same care you would choose soldiers to fight side by side with you in battle. Choose carefully, and you may be surprised how willing people are to help. You do not need to have a 5 hour long discourse with 4 people all at once, but you can certainly have a meaningful conversation with 1 or more over the grill, or at the mall waiting for your wives while they buy

God knows what candles from that weird shop that is probably a money laundering front. There will never be an absolute 'right time' to collaborate with people. You have to carve that time out and make the most of it. You may be surprised to find that many folks want to help, you just need to approach them with the need. Invite them in, assure them you will not badger them daily, and find out if they can assist. You can approach it like an interview process, why not. You will find they will typically make time to assist you. Avoid the ones that drink heavily, they may not make good barometers for your efforts.

If a group setting suits you, that's a strong option. A group can help a person evaluate their alcohol issues. They offer support, perspective, and accountability. Here are some excellent examples of ways a group can help you in your journey.

Sharing Perspectives

No two people are alike, except conjoined twins, and even they are not alike, really. Group members from different backgrounds can share diverse views on drinking behavior. This helps individuals better understand their habits and the possible outcomes. Each journey is unique. Hearing about others can help you feel validated in your own path to overcoming alcohol.

Providing Emotional Support

Group members should show empathy and validation. They should also encourage each other. This helps create a safe, non-judgmental space. In this environment, individuals can talk openly about their challenges and concerns with alcohol use. Remember, if you own 4 cats, that group of cats is not what we would consider a good group to be talking to about reducing or quitting, but if that is where you need to start, great. Just get around humans at some point in the very, very near future.

Offering Feedback

Groups can give helpful feedback based on what they see in someone's behavior. This can help identify patterns, triggers, and areas that need improvement. This is critical. More perspectives often lead to faster insight. Encourage your group to be blunt, honest, and constructively critical. A healthy feedback loop often produces more questions than answers, and that's a good sign. Growing your 'book of questions' to be answered means you are touching on more points. Be careful of analysis paralysis. Too much data can stall action. "Man, I have a lot of questions about how to quit drinking effectively, I just don't know where to start." is not a good analysis if you are trying to really quit. Digest your options, weigh those options and at some point, get moving in the direction of reducing or quitting by picking a starting point. You must start. You can pivot later.

Encouraging Reflection

Group discussions help individuals think about their main "whys"—their motivations, values, and goals around drinking. This boosts self-awareness and offers insights into their habits. Knowing your habits doesn't make them any less or more destructive. Be careful not to compare yourself to any one person. What you drink is your journey. You comparing yourself to someone could lead you down a path where you just continually think your drinking habits are 'fine' or 'normal' when they are not. It is your challenge. There are people that drink a pint a day of liquor or 24 beers a night, and there are people that have 1 glass of wine. It doesn't matter what the consumption is, what matters is the self-awareness of your personal drinking habits and what you personally want to do. Compare yourself to yourself, not the neighbor down the street.

Offering Resources

External resources can accelerate progress. You should seek a variety of outside resources to support your journey. Groups can share information, resources, and strategies to tackle alcohol-related issues. This includes self-help books, movies, support groups, counseling services, and treatment programs. If you're new to reducing or quitting alcohol, experienced people can help. They can suggest useful tools once they understand your situation better through conversation and details about your journey. If your Mom sends you your Dad's pistol, a la Hemingway, that is not a good resource. If your Mom buys you a few books about being sober, that is a good resource.

Providing Accountability

Group members can hold each other accountable for their goals about cutting back on alcohol. They can offer support and encouragement throughout the process. Accountability is critical in achieving any goal in life. You want results, you need to put in the work. Trusted group members will not penalize you for missing a goal, but rather assist on how to get you back on track. Try not to be too tough on yourself, thus causing additional unwanted stress and a possible relapse into old habits. Turn to motivational monikers, past successes, and a brighter future. Everyone screws up at some point whether they have 100% control over it or not. If you're sabotaging yourself, consider seeking more support. Your trusted group or mentors might not be enough. This is fair to both you and them.

Being accountable means more than just not drinking. It's about building relationships and trust. You also need to be honest about your successes and failures. There is nothing worse than the gambler who is quick to tell you they won $500 on the slot machines, but somehow conveniently forgets to tell you they spent $2,300 total to 'win' the $500. What the hell. Just come clean and earn respect for telling the truth. The reality is, most people do not want to be embarrassed. Moving your martini means to 'own it' and move on. Chalk up the mistake you made, learn from it, and try to avoid that mistake again.

Modeling Healthy Behaviors

Seeing others succeed can reinforce your belief that change is possible. These role models can motivate change in their own lives. If you see a group member as a role model, consider developing that into a mentorship. This can help you continue to emulate them for positive change.

Facilitating Referrals

Group members can help the individual find professional resources. This includes addiction counselors, therapists, or support groups. These connections can address underlying issues and build effective coping strategies. The internet is a great place, but nothing beats starting with folks you trust and getting their feedback on people that might be able to help you.

The right group can be invaluable. They help you assess and address issues related to alcohol consumption. Let the group be blunt and you will benefit more.

Continuous Improvement

The *5 Whys* technique aligns naturally with the principles of continuous improvement and lifelong learning. By repeatedly asking *why* and addressing root causes, you cultivate a mindset and a lifestyle that is focused on progress rather than reaction.

That said, resist the urge to broadcast your newfound analytical powers. Not everyone wants a detailed breakdown of how you've optimized every scenario. Improvement works best when it is internalized first. Do the work quietly. People will notice.

Yes, WD-40 solves many mechanical problems but not everyone wants a lecture about lubrication. Let your progress speak for itself.

Begin with the basics of self care:

- Keep your appearance neat. It doesn't cost you money to tuck a shirt in.
- Groom intentionally. Clean fingernails. Nails look good.
- Maintain fresh breath. Maintain is the key word.
- Wear clean shoes that are appropriate for the occasion.
- Keep your car and personal spaces tidy and clean.
- Engage a little secret called Feng Shui and unlock clarity and flow in your domicile and workspace.
- Carry a nicer pen, not some free piece of shit from the bank.

Continuous improvement is not a dramatic overhaul; it is disciplined consistency.

As you improve, you will find you are no longer 'attracted' to wanting to hang out in the same dingy environments. Those bars you go to - look around with the lights on - they are nasty. You might even paint a room in your house or apartment to get a completely different vibe and effect. Feng Shui research can lead to less clutter and better harmony in your everyday environment. Get a new lamp and watch how it transforms a room. It's amazing how something so simple can change the mood, look, and feel of a space. We are not saying run out and subscribe to Architectural Digest to outfit your living quarters, but for fucks sake, clean your bathroom and don't have toothpaste splatter all over the damn place because you brush your teeth like a neanderthal using the needles of a branch of a white pine tree. Start holding yourself accountable and become the improvement you visualize. Small steps can lead to a larger impact.

Take it one step at a time. You'll likely drift away from alcohol as you focus on new goals. Trying not to drink as you do these projects is important. Continuously improving by decreasing alcohol consumption requires commitment, effort, and a strategic approach.

Here are some steps you can take to gradually reduce your alcohol intake (continually improving) over time to zero.

Set Specific Goals

Define clear and achievable goals for reducing alcohol consumption. Begin with small, realistic goals. Limit drinks each week or skip alcohol on specific days. Pick the easiest days. The lower hanging fruit is going to give you quicker wins and help 'move the needle' faster.

Move the needle explained: To understand what it means to **"move the needle,"** think about a dial with a needle pointing towards different levels. If you want to make an impact, you need to move the needle significantly towards your desired outcome. In other words, you need to make substantial progress or change that will have a measurable impact on your goals. Imagine a dial: progress only counts when the needle visibly moves.

This idiom is often used in situations where incremental changes are not enough, and there is a need for significant progress. For example, if sales figures are stagnant, management may ask their team members to come up with ideas that will **"move the needle"** and increase revenue substantially.

In drinking, if you reduce your daily beer drinking count from 15 to 14, that is not really 'moving the needle.' But if you reduce the total count you consume, for example, from 15 beers to 8, you are moving the needle significantly.

Track progress in a way that lets you see it and, more importantly, celebrate it.

Track Consumption

Keep track of alcohol consumption using a journal, mobile app, or tracking tool. Tracking your daily or weekly intake can boost awareness of your drinking habits. It also helps you see how you're progressing toward your goals. An easy way to start is to only keep the actual number of beers you should drink in the fridge cold. No one wants a warm beer, well, almost no one. Make alcohol inconvenient and alternatives easy. Have that something else cold and ready to go. It might be a carbonated soft drink, an NA beer, or an ice cream bar.

Identify Triggers

Find triggers or situations that lead to drinking. These can include stress, social gatherings, or certain places. Create ways to handle triggers. Try finding new coping methods or staying away from risky situations. At first you may decline offers to participate in events that may involve drinking - a baseball game, a backyard BBQ, or a birthday celebration. If needed, decline the event, but work towards the goal of handling triggers as best as you can so you can attend the events you want. More key insights on this topic later.

Establish Boundaries

Limit your alcohol intake. Avoid places where alcohol is easy to get. Set a strict drink limit for social events. Use your support system to help you along this path where possible. Be proud and confident in your endeavor of reducing or not drinking alcohol. Confide in a trusted source to help you navigate your boundaries if possible. If stuck on a smaller boat and they only have alcohol to drink, you find yourself in a slight predicament, but alas, you can overcome it by declining the drinks and mustering through the event. Use your grit to gain the win!

Practice Mindfulness

Try mindfulness techniques to increase awareness of your thoughts, feelings, and actions related to drinking. Mindfulness can help individuals become more conscious of their choices and make intentional decisions about alcohol consumption. Meditation practices offer simple, effective tools. Don't get crazy, it's not about long haired hippies with dirty, long beards with birds living in the beard. It is about making the effort to not drink. Meditation can mean literally any sort of 'pause' in life's activities, no matter the length of time. When someone tells you to take a deep breath, that is what they are referring to. Taking a 10-30 second pause before acting or reacting is magnificent on many levels. It requires a conscious decision to pause, and a conscious effort to carry through the entire time. Fair warning, if you tell your wife to take a breath, she might knock your block off.

Mindfulness is more about intention and awareness of yourself. Does grabbing that drink have any immediate or near immediate impact on the immediate experience? Do you really need to juggle a drink and your task at hand? Should you really be drinking at all when you are doing the task at hand? Running that chainsaw and drinking cold beers because it is 98° outside is not the best idea, even if it is a small chainsaw. Moving your martini suggests not drinking during important events in order to better absorb what is actually happening. Take the classic soccer Mom drinking from her 'container of the moment' jug of a cocktail, wine, or spritzer. She does this to 'bide her time' and 'deal with' watching her kid play the sport at hand, missing out on a plethora of things, and most likely eventually making a fool of herself. She is 'too smart' and thinks she is getting away from it. Breaking news, everyone knows what she is doing, and commenting about it. Trust us.

We are here to tell you we are 100% positive TOO MANY Mom's do this. Maybe it's their social hour. How do we know? Because if they were sober, and saw how their kid REALLY played the sport of organized running, they would realize their kid is absolutely horrible at it and is really just learning how to suck at something and deal with it. Not the best outcome long term for the kid. Funny? Yes and no. So stop drinking while you fraternize with the other parents, assess what is really going on, and take it all in for the valuable activity that it is. Don't passively assuage yourself because your kid 'needs to be doing something' or the other parents talked you into it.

We could also discuss, ad nauseam and with some level of humor, the normalization of a Mom needing to have her 'wine time' after a busy day of watching kids. Don't buy into it. Never buy into it. The wine industry has done a great job convincing the Mother to relax with a glass or 4 of wine after a long day of being a Mom. What the fuck is that all about. There are plenty of other ways to reward yourself whilst not losing your shit on your kids because they are not respecting the coveted Mommy time. On top of it, this is what being a Mom is all about, and why we believe it is the greatest gift on earth. So, seek your intention for the night, give your kids things to do, and try not to resort to the glass of wine to unwind. Try morphing this into a sober routine and enjoy your kids.

Seek Support

Get help from friends, family, or support groups. They can provide encouragement, accountability, and understanding as you cut back on drinking.

Find Alternatives

Explore fun activities and hobbies that bring joy and satisfaction without alcohol. Here are some starter ideas:

- Try painting or drawing to express your creativity.
- Join a local sports team to stay active and meet new people.
- Take up gardening to connect with nature and enjoy fresh air.
- Learn to play a musical instrument for a rewarding challenge.
- Start a book club to share stories and ideas with friends.
- Explore cooking new recipes for a tasty adventure.
- Volunteer in your community to make a difference.
- Practice yoga or meditation for relaxation and wellness.

These options can help you enjoy life to the fullest without relying on alcohol. What is cool is possibly connecting with your kids or parents on some new hobbies, sharing a new language between each other, breathing new life into relationships.

Engage in activities such as exercise, hobbies, or socializing with non-drinking friends. While this sounds easy, it may not be. All too often people associate an activity with drinking and find it weird or unusual to not include alcohol. "What do we do for 4 hours?" is a common question relating to this. Work on developing a new set of skills and you should find that just the mere zig zag to a new skill requires things you didn't know. Don't confuse this with the Zig Zags at the local bodega by the way. If you never fished and all of sudden you want to take it up, get ready. There are so many variables it will make your head spin. Deep lake, Great Lakes, pond, river, marsh, brackish water, lowlands, highlands, etc. Who knew there were so many cool variables? Maybe Babe Winkleman, but really, it is great to learn new things and eventually, maybe share those new found discoveries with others.

Be present and in the moment. It is a journey and The Art of Sober wants you to take your time. Investing time into a hobby is the first step. Do you even find it remotely interesting? If you can afford a hobby, pursue it. We don't suggest going broke trying to replace drinking with a hobby, but we do encourage the replacement theory of replacing drinking with hobby. Fair warning, if you get into model trains as a hobby, it is cool as hell but can be big time $. We know.

Seek Professional Help

If cutting back on alcohol is hard, or if there are reasons behind your drinking, seek help. A healthcare professional, counselor, or addiction specialist can offer support. They can provide personalized guidance, resources, and treatment options to address alcohol-related issues effectively.

Celebrate Successes

Acknowledge and celebrate progress towards reducing alcohol consumption, no matter how small. A steak dinner, pedicure, pair of sunglasses, an expensive car wash, or a new pair of pants. Do it. Reward yourself for reaching milestones and achieving goals, reinforcing positive behavior change. We liken it to the reward receptors in the brain. The more rewards for good behavior, the more good behavior. This is the exact reason you might have gotten into heavy drinking. The more you drink, the better you think you feel. Turn the negative of drinking into the positive of sober.

Be Patient and Persistent

Understand that cutting back on alcohol takes time and may include setbacks and challenges. Be patient with yourself and remain committed to making positive changes over time. There will be peaks and valleys. Do not beat yourself up into oblivion for making a mistake. Talk to your support group about setbacks they may have experienced and get a better gauge on your own set of circumstances. We firmly believe that for the most part, you are not the first person to be dealing with a situation. Yes, there are exceptions, like testing the first nuclear bomb - they were literally the first people dealing with that, but it doesn't happen often.

Using these strategies and staying positive, you can reduce or stop drinking. This will help improve your health and well-being.

The 5 Whys technique is a useful tool. It helps with problem-solving, root cause analysis, and continuous improvement. This method can aid in reducing or avoiding alcohol use. It is coincidentally also applied frequently across various domains, including business, manufacturing, healthcare, and other personal development goals. Now that you are aware of this technique, let's move forward.

Roadblocks to the 5 Whys

If you keep asking yourself "why" and still don't arrive at clarity, that's okay. This process is not meant to be rushed.

Lack of Awareness

Many people are unaware of the true reasons behind their behavior. In such cases, it may be challenging to articulate the underlying motivations. Try to journal your frustrations and thoughts, identifying recurring themes in those thoughts. Zoom out and perform additional reflection. Let the ideas flow to you, without force. Bounce ideas off of trusted sources. Awareness rarely arrives as a lightning strike. That's normal.

Complexity of the Issue

Some problems are multifaceted, making a single root cause difficult to isolate. In these situations, the "why" question may lead to multiple contributing factors rather than a single underlying cause. This isn't a failure. It allows you to prioritize and address multiple contributing factors. It does happen. Journal your thoughts and make a genuine effort to categorize them into high and low priority. Assign each issue a simple priority rating (for example, 1–4) and address them at your own pace. Think about the most important issues you want to tackle first. Focus on addressing each one step by step.

Emotional or Psychological Barriers

Some issues are tied to emotions, past experiences, or psychological factors. This can make it hard to find the real reasons just by asking questions. Talking to a therapist or counselor can help with these complex issues. Distinguish between issues that require professional support and those amplified by temporary emotion or self-importance. Beginning with a professional can be a worthwhile investment.

Resistance or Denial

People might avoid looking into some of their actions or beliefs. This can make it difficult to grasp the "why." This resistance may stem from fear, shame, or reluctance to confront uncomfortable truths.

In summary, if you struggle to understand your "why," approach the process with patience, openness, and reflection. Explore the issue from various angles. Seek input from trusted friends, family, or professionals. Also, practice mindfulness or journaling. This can help you better understand your thoughts, feelings, and behaviors. Rome was not built in a day. Also, be kind to yourself during this process. Finding your true motivations takes time and may need help from others.

Many people stop this exercise too soon. They often quit before reaching the point where asking "why" five times leads to real results. Gain internal and external feedback if needed to structure your 5 whys. It doesn't need to be perfect—only meaningful enough to sustain. It may take a day, it may take a month. You may rewrite the question or reframe it many times before you settle on the wording. At some point, stop, frame it, and move on to the next one.

It is completely normal to lack an opinion on something you do not understand. That is ok. Having competing thoughts is ok too. You cannot be a genius in everything. Do not let being right become an epidemic you have to deal with in this exercise. The fact that you are doing it at all is progress.

Alternative methods to the 5 Whys

If the 5 Whys don't work for you, other root cause analysis methods may help. You can find the root cause and solutions for cutting alcohol from your life. Just ask questions several times. We will cover them in a basic format. If one resonates, do some research on the methodology and discover how it can assist your journey.

Basic Root Cause Analysis Method

Root Cause Analysis (RCA) forms the foundation of the 5 Whys. It also offers more technical analysis options beyond the 5 Whys. It looks at events leading to the problem. Then, it identifies immediate causes and digs deeper to find root causes. Techniques like fishbone diagrams and fault tree analysis can help. Try using one of these tools to help you visualize quitting alcohol. This can be useful if answering the 5 why's feels tough for you.

When thinking about why someone drinks, remember that each person's situation and experiences are different. As an illustrative exercise, here are some potential detailed root causes for why a person may drink excessively:

Underlying Trauma or Emotional Pain

Past trauma such physical, emotional, or sexual abuse can drive people to use alcohol. They often do this to numb their emotional pain or distress. Write these down and see what needs to be addressed to provide the highest impact to less drinking.

Mental Health Disorders

Co-occurring mental health issues like depression, anxiety, bipolar disorder, and PTSD can lead to heavy drinking. People often use alcohol to self-medicate and ease their symptoms. We cannot say this enough, if you are having strong feelings of suicide, CALL 911. There is help.

Genetic Predisposition

Some people may be genetically prone to alcoholism or addiction. This can make it easier for them to develop harmful drinking habits.

Social or Peer Pressure

Peer pressure and social norms about drinking can push people to drink too much. They may do this to fit in, feel accepted, or meet others' expectations. Younger people tend to deal with this frequently. Learning how to manage this sooner than later will help you gain an edge of not drinking.

Stress or Pressure

High stress from work, school, or relationships can lead people to drink. They may use alcohol to cope or escape overwhelming situations. Overcoming stress can start with finding bigger problems than what you currently think are problems. Solve each problem as you move forward. Address the compression of an issue and resolve it.

Boredom or Lack of Fulfillment

Boredom, emptiness, or feeling unfulfilled can push people to seek excitement. They often turn to alcohol for stimulation. Fill your vacuum with planned activities you have at the ready when there is downtime, such as a walk or call to your Mom!

Family or Environmental Factors

Growing up in an environment where excessive drinking is normalized or having family members with a history of alcoholism can increase the likelihood of developing problematic drinking habits. The classic follow the leader syndrome, but the reality is, you need to become your own leader. Many folks see successful people drinking and safely assume, if they can do it, I can too. The potential reality is, you are not with that person 100% of the time. They could be scaling it back while in your presence, and be a raging drinker when no one is looking - happens all the time. Success, loosely defined, does not equate to sobriety directly or indirectly. It is independent of each other. Sober as a state of success sits on its own. We know very wealthy people that are chronic relapse types. They are successful by many measures, except sober. Define your idea of success, then get there.

Lack of Coping Skills

Some people may not have good ways to cope with stress or emotions. Because of this, they might rely on alcohol to handle tough situations.

Social Anxiety or Insecurity

People might drink alcohol to ease social anxiety, feel more confident, or hide their insecurities in social settings. Liquid courage is the name. New to the union hall meeting? Drinking definitely happening.

Unhealthy Coping Mechanisms

People who lack healthy coping skills may use alcohol to deal with life challenges or negative feelings.

Approach your root cause assessment with sensitivity and empathy. Remember, everyone's situation is unique and complex, so stay non-judgmental. Getting help from healthcare pros, counselors, or support groups can help people face underlying issues. It also helps them build better ways to cope with alcohol use.

Cause and Effect Analysis Method

Cause-and-effect analysis—also known as the *Fishbone Diagram* or *Ishikawa Diagram*—visually maps the potential causes of a problem in a structured way. It organizes causes into categories such as people, process, environment, and management in order to help identify root drivers. Picture a fishbone-shaped diagram: the head represents the problem, and the branching bones represent contributing categories and factors. If this approach resonates, a brief review of the method can deepen its usefulness.

Here's a simple way to apply it:

Identify the Problem

Begin by clearly defining the behavior you want to examine and place it at the head of the diagram. Examples might include:

- I drink every Sunday night.
- I drink 1 cocktail every night during the weekday.

- I drink when my newborn has a nasty diaper blowout.
- I drink when the sky is blue.

Define the behavior honestly, without minimizing or justifying it

Identify Categories of Causes

Next, draw the backbone of the diagram and label broad categories of potential causes.

Most common categories include:

- People
- Work events
- Social anxiety
- Enablers
- The need to drink when smoking
- Relationships
- Work
- Social environment
- Family

Brainstorm Potential Causes

For each category, brainstorm potential causes or factors that could contribute to the problem. Write these causes as branches extending from the backbone. Examples might include: alcohol is readily available; my company pays for happy hour; a family member always brings beer over; social identity around wine or whiskey; or an inability to watch sports without drinking.

Analyze Relationships

Once you've identified potential causes, you can analyze the relationships between them and the problem. Some causes will be direct triggers, while others act more subtly in the background.

A mandatory after-work event with an open bar will almost certainly lead to drinking. An after work meet up with some co-workers on a Tuesday night you skipped (a school night as they say) where they are trash talking on you about watching reruns of Friends, and you find out, via text, whilst sitting at home, watching a rerun of *Friends*, may indirectly lead you to drink at home after receiving a text that triggers resentment or exclusion.

Identify Root Causes

Use the diagram to isolate root causes. These are the factors that, if addressed, can significantly reduce recurrence.

By visually organizing causes, fishbone analysis allows you to systematically examine contributing factors and identify areas for action. It encourages perspective, creativity, and a more nuanced understanding of alcohol use. The ultimate goal is to reduce or eliminate alcohol's control over your behavior.

We have included a workbook exercise for you, use it as you see fit

---

Cause-and-Effect (Fishbone) Workbook Exercise

Understanding Why You Drink — So You Can Change It

Purpose: This exercise helps you identify the **real drivers behind your drinking habits**. Instead of relying on willpower or vague intentions, you'll visually map **causes, triggers, and patterns** so you can intervene where it actually matters.

Take your time. This is about **clarity**, not perfection

Step 1: Define the Behavior (The "Head" of the Fish)

Write **one specific drinking behavior** you want to understand or change. Examples:

- "I drink every Sunday night."
- "I have a cocktail every weekday evening."
- "I drink when I feel excluded or stressed."
- "I drink automatically when relaxing at home."

My behavior:

Be honest. This is for you—not for judgment.

Step 2: Identify High-Level Cause Categories (The "Bones")

Below are common categories. Check the ones that apply to you and add others if needed.

☐ People / Relationships
☐ Work / Career
☐ Social Environment
☐ Emotional States (stress, anxiety, boredom, loneliness)
☐ Habits & Pairings (sports, smoking, cooking, TV)
☐ Family Influence
☐ Availability / Convenience
☐ Identity or Self-Image
☐   Other:

Step 3: Brainstorm Contributing Causes

For each category you selected, list **specific causes** that apply to *you*.

Category: _______________________________

✍ Cause(s):

- ____
- ____

Category: _______________________________

✍ Cause(s):

- ____
- ____

Category: _______________________________

✍ Cause(s):

- ____
- ____

Write freely. Use the space below for note taking.

Step 4: Identify Direct vs. Indirect Causes

Review what you wrote and mark each cause:

- **D** = Direct trigger (almost always leads to drinking)
- **I** = Indirect influence (sets the stage)

Example:

- "Open bar at work events" → **D**
- "Feeling left out socially" → **I**

✍ Re-label your causes above with **D** or **I**.

Step 5: Identify Root Causes

Now answer this honestly:

If I could change only ONE or TWO of these causes, which would most reduce my drinking?

Root Cause #1:

✍ ____

Root Cause #2 (if applicable):

✍ ____

These are leverage points—not everything needs fixing at once

Step 6: Reality Check

Answer briefly:

- Is this cause **within my control** right now? ☐ Yes ☐ Partially ☐ No
- If not, what *is* within my control?

✍ ____

Step 7: One Small Intervention

Choose **one realistic action** you can take this week to interrupt a root cause.

Example:

- Skip one recurring drinking event
- Change the environment (availability, timing, routine)
- Replace the habit pairing
- Introduce friction (delay, substitute, pause)

My action:

✍ ____

When will I do it?

✍ ____

Step 8: Reflection (Optional But Powerful)

After one week, answer:

- What changed?
- What surprised me?
- What didn't work—and why?

Reminder: This exercise is not about blame. It's about **pattern recognition and agency**. You are not broken. You are learning how your system works.

Repeat this process as needed. Each pass sharpens awareness and weakens automatic behavior. Moving on to more method options.

Pareto Analysis Method

Pareto Analysis—often called the **80/20 Rule**—helps you identify the few drivers that create most of your consequences. You rank triggers by frequency and impact, then focus on the ones that do the most damage.

The principle is simple: a small number of causes often produce a disproportionate share of outcomes. Applied to drinking, a handful of moments such as specific nights, places, people, or emotions, may create most of the fallout.

Here's what that can look like:

The 20% (The Trigger):

One Monday night. Football, a night out—whatever the event. You have a few drinks, drive home, and tell yourself you got away with it. You scrape the car while parking. You come in hot, misplace your keys, snap at the barking dog, and wake the kids while trying to make late-night pizza rolls. You go to bed irritated.

The 80% (The Consequences):
The oven's left on. The food burns to a black crisp. The house stinks. The kids are cranky from being woken up in the middle of the night and lost sleep. The dog shits a mess because you didn't take it out. Morning is chaos: you can't find your keys, you're late, and you get pulled over because the taillight is out. And your mind still tries to call it a win: *At least I didn't get a DUI.*

Your Move:
List the handful of drinking situations that create most of your problems. Rank them by impact. Then pick **one** to interrupt this week—through avoidance, substitution, or a new boundary.

Rank what is causing the 80% of all your issues you have. Meditate on that, write them down, and start working on reducing these issues.

It is a modern statistic that in the USA, 10-20% of the drinkers consume about 75% of the alcohol sold, averaging about 74 drinks per week. Holy shit. You think today, to yourself, that you don't drink nearly that much, so all is well. Time. Time has you. You bought the ticket, you are on the ride. Time to get off the ride.

Failure Mode and Effects Analysis (FMEA) Method
FMEA is a proactive technique for identifying and mitigating potential failures or risks in a system, process, or product. It involves systematically analyzing failure modes, their effects, and potential causes to prioritize preventive actions. That is the textbook definition.

In real life, FMEA comes down to a simple truth: actions create predictable reactions. Over time, repeated behaviors produce the same outcomes. Eventually, even those reactions fade. Once that starts happening, you most likely are approaching or have hit rock bottom. This is a system widely used in manufacturing, now we apply it to drinking.

A clear example is alcohol tolerance. Your first beer when you are 13 years old reacts to you in a way that differs significantly from your first beer on a Tuesday night, 16 years later, due to the buildup of tolerance and other factors.

Here's how this unfolds over time. You carry out an action, such as drinking too much in one night. You come home. In the early stages of doing this, people engaged you when you came home. They might have asked you how the night was, were worried, tried to help you get to bed, etc. As this repeats, help quietly disappears often without you noticing. You stumble in, look around and see no one. Those people want nothing to do with you. You are doing this to yourself. They don't get out of bed and help you as you stumble around the kitchen. They don't get you a glass of water. They just don't give a shit. That withdrawal is often a warning sign. You are approaching rock bottom. Avoid that sooner than later.

Each incident is a preventable failure point. Each effect is something you can interrupt. Let's take a moment to illustrate in painful detail how these failures can impact various age groups and life stages. See where you are today, and visualize what could happen if you do not start making changes to become the sober you. Visualize

21-50 Year Olds
Health Problems
Drinking too much can lead to many health problems. These include liver disease, heart issues, digestive troubles, brain damage, a weakened

immune system, and higher chances of some cancers. These health problems can significantly impact quality of life and longevity. No shit.

Addiction and Dependence

Excessive drinking can lead to alcohol addiction or dependence. It changes your 'voltage' over time. At a younger age, you are high voltage. Drinking will lower your voltage over time. Addiction means you may crave alcohol strongly and lose control over your drinking. You might also experience withdrawal symptoms if you try to cut back or stop. Alcohol addiction can have profound effects on relationships, employment, and overall well-being. It may start at 21 or it may start at a later date.

Impaired Judgment

Drinking too much alcohol can mess with your judgment. This can lead to bad choices in many areas, like relationships, money, work, and safety. This can result in damaged relationships, financial instability, job loss, and legal troubles. This will cost you money undoubtedly.

Reduced Productivity

Alcohol abuse can lower productivity at work or school. This happens because of absenteeism, tardiness, lack of focus, and poor cognitive function. This can hinder career advancement opportunities and negatively impact earning potential.

Financial Hardship

Excessive drinking can lead to high costs. You spend money on alcohol. There are also healthcare expenses for alcohol-related health issues. Legal fees for DUI charges can add up, too. Plus, you might lose income from being unemployed or underemployed.

Family and Relationship Problems

Alcohol abuse can strain relationships with family members, friends, romantic partners, and co-workers. It can cause conflicts, arguments, and emotional distance. This leads to poor communication and feelings of isolation, loneliness, and alienation. The situation worsens when multiple people are drinking heavily together. To the group, it is business as usual - the commenting, the loud obnoxious behavior, the firework that goes off in the wrong direction and flattening your Mom to the ground upon impact to the chest with a massive mortar. To a sober observer, it often looks like chaos.

Try to attend a larger event and either don't drink or reduce it to a level you can analyze, as an outsider, what is going on. You will notice people talking to you but their eyes are crossed and unfocused. You will no doubt encounter one or more inebriated people that 'heavy hugs' you and says 'I love you, man' over and over. It drones on when you are sober. When you are sky high in Margaritaville, it is 100% normal behavior. We won't even talk about the person who lobs out a 'deep thought' and talks about it for 2 hours to whoever will listen. Ahhh, family dynamics. Don't ditch your family, just maybe tone it down over time and see what transpires.

Parenting Challenges

Excessive drinking can disrupt parenting. It may lead to neglect, inconsistent discipline, and weakened caregiving skills. Children of parents who abuse alcohol can face emotional, psychological, and developmental issues because of it. We cannot say the kids will follow in your footsteps, but, monkey see, monkey do (MSMD). This strongly resonates with many of the parental choices. Tattoos - MSMD. Piercings - MSMD. Unplanned pregnancies in a not so ideal situation - MSMD. Run in with the police - MSMD. Anger management. MSMD. MSMD might just be your new favorite acronym to identify not so beneficial behaviors. The same goes for healthy behavior. A parent who works out routinely and is physically fit? The child most likely will too. MSMD is a lifestyle when raising kids. Know this.

Physical and Mental Health Decline

Excessive drinking can speed up the decline of both physical and mental health. It worsens existing health issues and raises the risk of new ones. Chronic alcohol abuse can cause depression, anxiety, insomnia, memory issues, and other mental health problems. You may want to consult a professional if you suspect serious health issues.

Legal Problems and a Quick Story

Alcohol-related offenses include DUI (driving under the influence), public intoxication, and disorderly conduct. Others are assault and property damage. These actions can lead to legal consequences like fines, probation, community service, license suspension, or even jail time. Sometimes you get into trouble and you get out of trouble with minimal scratches. Sometimes you get into a prolonged amount of systemic trouble.

One such legal incident was when the Chicago Bulls were playing for the NBA championship game. It was a weekday, so our usual crew were hunkered down at the abode 'studying' whilst watching the game.

The Bulls won and the city went berserk. Every bar in our neighborhood let out and people were cheering and shouting as loud as they could. Car horns blaring, and some fireworks going off. Triggered, I remembered I had some nice, powerful whistle and report bottlerockets stashed away. I am in my flip flops, shorts, t-shirt and on my front porch just lighting a bottle rocket that is resting horizontal on the concrete ledge. Why? I'm ten beers in and just soaking up the championship vibe. Michael Jordan never knew this celebration happened. I light the ever so potent bottle rocket. It gleefully launches off the ledge, familiar flames shooting out and I am part of the winning team celebrations! It zips across the street and hits the trunk of a newer Mercedes. A big black skid marks the car. Then, it lands in front of two beat cops patrolling the dark neighborhood. Stunned, they look around, the bottle rocket then explodes in front of them with a flash of light as bright as what you would imagine coming to the Pearly Gates would look like. I'm fucked. They point at little innocent me. I put my hands up. Off to the paddy wagon.

I am in the front section of the hot iron oven box of the paddy wagon, 10:30pm, handcuffed hard. Skinny, drunk, locked down and we drive off, heading to the main area in the neighborhood where ALL, and I mean ALL of the action is happening. Armitage and Halsted in the 90's. There are thousands of people in the streets and it is a cacophony of noise you cannot imagine. But alas, I am safe in the paddy wagon, but melancholy because I am missing the festivities with the multitudes of other drunk folk.

I guess none of them were really getting out of hand as the paddy wagon was still only filled to the brim with little old me. Then, one by one, as the clock ticked later into the night, the wagon door would swing open, police would toss in some meat, and close up the doors. These new roommates of mine were as drunk as drunk gets. Two latino gentlemen were tossed in with no handcuffs, huge builds and yelling at the top of their lungs some insane shit in Mexican, not Spanish. Mexican. I am now, 3 hours later, sober as sober gets. I just meek into my corner hoping a fight doesn't break out in the Mad Max PaddyDome. I just knew I would be the 'chum' they toss into the middle to get the 15 guys riled up before the main event.

I then realized, to my horror, that tomorrow I have my first day at my new job at 10am. I strategize that I have plenty of time to get let out later, get home, which is still a few blocks away, and get rested for work the next day. Surely they are going to hold us and release us there, most likely at 4am. I am the meek man in the corner, regretting decisions. Legal issues are not even crossing my mind.

At some point, in the middle of the night, the paddywagon actually starts to move. We are driven for what seems like 40 minutes due to the continued parade of people up and down out in the streets of Chicago at 2-3am, I am not sure. Finally the PaddyDome is stopping. I am thrilled I have not been pounded into paillard chicken by all the unhandcuffed roommates I have in the wagon. Luckily, it turns out they all aligned their hatred for the cops and fandom for the Bulls into a harmonious sing song of delight. I was aligned with getting the fuck out of the PaddyDome wagon in one piece.

At the police station, we went to the holding cell area. For ease of police work, we each get marked with four digits. I have 4848 on my right hand. Then, we are put into smaller holding cells to "wear off" the night. No communication from any authorities. Just shoved in and given a look of 'shut up'. My cellmate comes crawling from out under the metal-slab bed, slinkies himself up using the bars as support, and just stares at me. Not too crazy, except when his face unblurred in the dark of night and he looked exactly like Charles Manson. No small talk ensued, as the plan with my new roommate was for me to get to bed. I figured he slinked out from under the bed, he can slink back under the bed. I took the death metal bed

Daylight arrives and the cops open the doors, filing us out neatly into the blistering hot daylight of the cellblock room. I find my bearings and the time and realize I have 40 minutes to get to my first day on the new job. As I am chugging along, out of shape, to my job, I see the 4848 emblazoned on my hand. I have to look presentable at my first job. I begin to hawk tuah on my hand and rub it off as best as I can. There is still faint writing, but it just looks like I might have been at a club or something to that effect. I am now approaching T-2 city blocks home to do a quick change of clothes. I am golden and things seem to be working in my favor, albeit heavily breathing. I waltz the rest of the way, catching my breath. I swing the door open and lock eyes with my new manager, giving a hello type wave. All is good, I am on time and ready to work, forgetting the night.

We head to the nearest table to go over some light paperwork and what the day will look like. As we sit down, he points his pen at my hand and with a grin says, "How was jail last night?"

Loss of Opportunities

Excessive drinking can cause missed chances for personal and professional growth. It also reduces the ability to reach long-term goals and dreams. It can limit educational attainment, career advancement, and overall life satisfaction. Work or academic functions might seem like a natural place to imbibe. DO NOT DO IT.

Personal failures aren't a given with alcohol. Many times, people think the more successful they are, the more they can drink. We know plenty of well off folks that imbibe. Some responsibly, some not. People can seek help, make positive changes, and overcome the challenges of excessive drinking. Getting help from healthcare professionals, counselors, support groups, or rehab programs is the first step to recovery. It's key to rebuilding a healthy and fulfilling life

50-80 Year Olds

Below are common failures and consequences of excessive drinking for adults ages 50–80. These patterns can create serious health, relationship, and financial consequences. Common impacts include:

Health Problems

Excessive drinking can cause outsized health problems. These include liver disease, heart issues, and cognitive impairment. It can also raise the risk of some cancers, lead to digestive disorders, and weaken the immune system. Additionally, weight is a constant battle for many folks. Alcohol is empty calories. A short daily walk—ten minutes to start—can make a measurable difference. Not as fast as when you were 25, but there will be changes.

Relationship Strain

Excessive drinking can strain relationships with family members, friends, and romantic partners. It fuels conflicts. Trust may be lost, leading to feelings of resentment or isolation among loved ones. If you have grandchildren, protect and fortify that bond. They are gifts, unless they are hellions and mooch off of you.

Financial Instability

Alcohol misuse can cause financial problems. Buying alcohol adds up. There are also medical costs from health issues linked to drinking. Legal fees can pile up big time. Plus, it can lead to lost income or job opportunities. In your journal, track what you spend on alcohol each week. Don't risk losing a job to booze.

Social Isolation

Excessive drinking can lead to social isolation. It may cause people to withdraw from activities, hobbies, and community events. This often leads to loneliness and a sense of disconnection from others.It often intensifies after the loss of a spouse. We suggest joining groups where possible. Hanging out at the strip club, maybe not great. A motorcycle gang's clubhouse might not sound like the best use of time, but you may find it is genuine, beneficial, and rewarding. You do you. Try a church group, volunteering at an animal shelter, a vintage car club, or a weekly card game. The cold reality is this: you are going to die. Everyone does. SPEND your money on you! You earned it, you should enjoy it. Time is finite. Go take that vacation, alone if need be. Go to that nice dinner with your grandkids more frequently. Don't wait for someone to call, you call them. Create memories because at the end of your time, you should want people to retell great stories about you, not about how you withdrew from everything you cared about. You can learn behaviors that get you out and about. Just go do it. We cannot stress this enough. They say you only live once. That is 100% false. You only die once, you live every day.

Decline in Cognitive Function

Drinking too much alcohol can harm your brain. It affects memory and makes it hard to concentrate. You may struggle with decisions and problem-solving, hurting your overall thinking skills. Be aware alcohol can really increase your cognitive decline faster than you can say the Woodchuck jingle. Do not lower your voltage!

Neglect of Responsibilities

Excessive drinking may lead to neglect of responsibilities at home, work, or in the community. People might find it hard to meet their duties. This can cause issues like skipping household chores, missing deadlines, or overlooking caregiving tasks. Be very careful with this, as lapses in things such as paying your life insurance bills could affect your estate plans. We have seen that first hand. There are many issues surrounding neglect of responsibilities. Ask a trusted family member or friend to help you stay organized. It is a strong person who asks others to help them stay in their proverbial guard rails. In the right setting, asking a loved one how your drinking affects them can reveal a powerful 'why.' If you hoard bad, you might need pro help!

Emotional and Mental Health Challenges

Drinking too much can worsen or cause emotional and mental health issues. These include depression, anxiety, mood swings, and low self-esteem. People might feel guilt, shame, disconnection, or hopelessness because of their drinking habits. It is never too late to reclaim control of your life, no matter your age.

Loss of Independence

Alcohol-related health issues or accidents can cause a loss of independence. This often makes individuals depend on others for care and support. This loss of independence can be emotionally distressing and impact individuals' sense of self-worth and dignity. This may be the most frightening consequence. Your children will put you in a nursing home faster than a bunny rabbit reproducing if you are causing them problems in their daily routines. Stop drinking and show them you can piddle around your house with the best of them, cleaning, cooking, taking care of the fake plants and more. We kid. Be independent by reducing or not drinking, which can disrupt your daily grind. Be sure to not watch the news all day. Pick an author or a favorite TV series. Build a daily structure that keeps you engaged and interested. May we also suggest rewatching old movies or TV shows from your earlier years, just to bring back a plethora of old memories. There are many books and psychological studies on this topic alone. If you tell a Grandkid born after 1985 that you love watching Buckwheat and Alfalfa, they are going to think you are batshit crazy. Be sure to clarify they were characters in the show *The Little Rascals* from back in the day. Who doesn't love that show, O'Tay!

Final Thoughts of Life Stages

Excessive drinking can and will greatly lower a person's quality of life, their voltage. It impacts physical health, mental well-being, relationships, finances, and overall happiness. At any age, the pattern can be changed with support. Seeking support from healthcare family, professionals, counselors, or support groups is vital. These resources can help address underlying issues, overcome barriers, and foster recovery and better well-being. If you need help, ask. It's a sign of strength. Let's continue with more valuable methods to getting sober.

Group Brainstorming Root Cause Method

Brainstorming is a simple, effective way to involve a few trusted people in identifying the root causes of your drinking and exploring solutions together. By inviting different perspectives, you often uncover factors you can't see on your own. You control the group size, pace, and structure of the conversation. You can keep it focused—or allow it to move into unfamiliar territory that may challenge you. The more you face what's unknown, the clearer it becomes. Be bold in recovery and become sober. Fortune favors the bold, risk-on person. Not taking a risk to become sober is not investing in yourself.

Set the Stage

Choose a time when everyone involved is calm and free from distractions. Approach the conversation with empathy, curiosity, and a nonjudgmental mindset. Keep the phones in a bin. Be purposeful.

Express Concern

Begin by sharing your concerns about your well-being and how drinking may be affecting your life or relationships. Use "I" statements rather than blame. Go slow. Pace the discussion.

Share Observations

Offer specific examples or incidents that have raised concern about your drinking. Stick to facts and avoid assumptions. Be open to direct honesty. It's often where real breakthroughs happen.

Encourage Openness

Invite others to share their thoughts and experiences with alcohol. Make it clear the goal is mutual listening and support, without judgment. When ideas are shared openly, insight follows.

Breaking the Ice

Ask people what nickname they have for you. Everyone has one. If it's uncomfortable, notice that. It's usually more awkward to say to someone's face than the receiver to hear. Embrace it and move forward. If it's vulgar, great. If it's innocent, great. If it reflects the truth, great. If it makes you sound like a fool, vote to get a new one!

Explore Motivations

Examine why you drink and how alcohol affects your life and relationships. Listen carefully to others' perspectives. Allow the conversation to deepen naturally. If it gets "stuck" on one topic, that's often a sign something important is worth exploring further.

Discuss Consequences

Consider both short- and long-term effects of alcohol use:

- **Short-term:** impaired judgment, accidents, mood swings
- **Long-term:** chronic health issues, mental health challenges, strained relationships
- **Overall:** reduced quality of life, difficulty maintaining responsibilities, isolation

Some consequences are obvious; others take time to surface.

Brainstorm Solutions

Work together to identify practical strategies—professional support, peer groups, clear limits, or healthier coping mechanisms. Focus on what feels achievable.

Offer Support

Support can come from a spouse, sibling, parent, child, or close friend. Presence matters. Knowing someone is willing to walk alongside you, attending appointments, checking in, or simply listening, can make progress feel possible.

Set Boundaries

Establish clear expectations around alcohol use. Respect what others can and cannot accept, and communicate boundaries clearly. Don't undermine them by drinking "around the corner" first. You know better now. Stop hiding your habit, conquer it.

Create a Follow-Up Plan

Agree on how you'll stay connected. Follow-up may fade over time, but keeping communication open matters most. Make it mutual and ongoing. Not just about drinking, but about life.

Addressing alcohol use is a process, not a single conversation. Change takes time. Stay patient, stay honest, and keep moving forward. If needed, a therapist, counselor, or addiction specialist can help guide the work and provide structure when things feel overwhelming.

You're not doing this to be perfect. You're doing it to be better. You are betting on yourself. Buy the ticket, take the ride!

Critical Incident Technique (CIT) Method

The Critical Incident Technique (CIT) asks you to examine *specific moments*—the nights, the arguments, the near-misses—and study them closely enough to see what actually drove your drinking. These real-life snapshots reveal patterns. Patterns give you leverage.

CIT is a qualitative method used to analyze pivotal incidents and their impact. When you apply it to alcohol use, focus on the factors below.

Nature of the Incident

Describe what happened, when and where it happened, and who was there. Whether it's a car accident, a fall, a blackout, or a missed commitment, get concrete. Vague stories protect the habit; details expose it.

Contextual Factors

Zoom out. What was happening around you that day. Maybe stress, conflict, celebration, boredom, loneliness? What did you have access to? Who was present? What trigger lit the fuse?

Individual Factors

Consider the people involved, including you: your state of mind, your history, your stress level, and any underlying issues (anxiety, depression, grief, trauma, dependence). Identify enablers, too. If certain environments or relationships repeatedly pull you toward drinking, that's data—not destiny, but data.

Perceptions and Experiences

Capture what you felt and believed in the moment. Before, during, and after are all critical. If others witnessed the incident, consider how they experienced it, and what it changed for them.

Coping Strategies and Responses

What did you do to cope? Helpful or harmful, conscious or automatic. Then write it down. Did you reach for support, or reach for the bottle? Did you avoid, numb, escalate, perform, disappear?

Outcomes and Resolution

Document what happened afterward. What could be immediate consequences and long-tail effects. If there were legal or work-related consequences, name them plainly. Then go one step further: visualize what *could* have happened if the night had gone slightly worse. This isn't catastrophizing—it's prevention.

Patterns and Trends

After you analyze multiple incidents, look for repeats: the same triggers, the same settings, the same cast of characters, the same "story" you tell yourself right before you drink. Those repeats are your intervention points.

Used well, CIT turns chaos into a map. Once you can see the sequence—trigger, context, choice, consequence—you can start interrupting it on purpose.

Your Personal Energy Flow Stack Analysis

We now look at your energies and its wear and tear on you.

Potential Energy (a Metaphor)

This refers to the energy you carry in relation to your environment and the internal stresses you hold. In simple terms, it reflects how forces act on you based on where you start and where you end up. This is your baseline state before alcohol enters the picture. This potential energy is stable and self-contained. It exists without outside interference. Introduce alcohol—an external chemical energy—into the system. That introduction converts stored energy into motion. Get ready for the ride. From here on, momentum takes over.

Chemical

The booze you drink affects your emotions and energy. It can make you want to dance, fight, daydream, or even act like a rodeo clown at a wedding. There are songs upon songs about this feeling. Our theory can be best described via the lyrics of "Cracklin' Rosie" by Neil Diamond. The lyrics are exactly about this chemical reaction. Plenty of other songs glorify substance abuse. So much so, you wish Tipper Gore was back in politics harassing these artists like she did Frank Zappa. It is perverse as hell, and no one gives one iota fuck about the content. It is as if it is being done by design. Let's revisit this chapter in 2075AD and see where we are at. Nonetheless, the chemical energy is the alcohol (or any other narcotic or substance really). Call it 'applied chemical' energy. Moving on.

Kinetic

This is where it gets fun, mental, insane, bionic, etc. Tops off, titties flashing at a Guns and Roses concert, bats getting their heads bitten off by Ozzy, Lady Gaga wearing a total red meat steak outfit, Charlie Sheen 'winning', Hunter Biden filming, people throwing chairs off rooftops, and so much more, all brought to you by substance abuse in motion. This highway is littered with actions that were fueled or influenced in some way, shape, or form, by booze.

Kinetic energy is energy in motion. It is what happens after potential energy is disturbed, when balance gives way to movement.

Once alcohol is introduced, the system no longer remains static. The body and mind shift from a state of contained readiness into action. Thoughts accelerate. Emotions loosen. Behavior follows. What was once internal becomes external.

This is where drinking begins to *feel* like something is happening.

In physics, kinetic energy increases with mass and velocity. In human terms, the parallel is simple: the more frequently and intensely alcohol is introduced, the greater the momentum it creates. One drink may create a subtle shift. Repeated drinks compound the effect. Over time, the motion becomes familiar, even expected.

The danger of kinetic energy is not movement itself—it is **unchecked movement**.

When alcohol-driven motion becomes habitual, decisions start occurring faster than reflection. Reactions replace intention. You move before you think. You speak before you listen. You act before you assess consequences. The system is no longer guided by awareness; it is guided by inertia.

This is why the early days of drinking often feel productive, social, or even clarifying. Motion feels like progress. Energy feels like confidence. But movement without direction is not growth, it is drift.

Left unexamined, kinetic energy seeks efficiency. The body and brain learn shortcuts. Alcohol becomes the fastest way to change states: from stress to relief, from boredom to stimulation, from anxiety to numbness. Over time, the system defaults to motion rather than choice. Eventually, stopping feels harder than continuing.

At this stage, drinking is no longer about escape or celebration. It is about maintaining momentum. Slowing down feels uncomfortable. Stillness feels unfamiliar. The idea of returning to potential energy, the quiet, contained, deliberate, can feel threatening.

But kinetic energy is not permanent. In physics, motion can be redirected, slowed, or transformed. The same is true here. Awareness introduces friction. Reflection reduces velocity. Choice reclaims direction. Reducing or removing alcohol does not eliminate energy, it converts it. The motion that once scattered attention can be harnessed. The speed that once led to mistakes can be redirected toward clarity, discipline, and intention.

Kinetic energy is powerful. When guided, it becomes progress. When ignored, it becomes chaos. The goal is not to eliminate motion, but to regain control over it.

Picture it. An example.

You drive thirty minutes into town to a pickup spot, let's say the Hyatt hotel, where you're meeting eight friends for a pre-wedding night out. At 5:00 p.m. sharp, a kick ass super stretch rock star worthy limo rolls up like destiny on wheels.

Inside: beers, bottled libations, and the immediate abandonment of indoor voices. Someone cracks one open. Then everyone does. Volume jumps from *polite Peter Gabriel* to *full stadium encore* in under sixty seconds. You think to yourself, I have the touch. You always do.

So far, so good.

The limo drops you at the coolest new bar in town in *Any Town, USA*. Your friends are single, seasoned, and socially insured. No lines. No bad service. No waiting. You're VIP by association. A gaggle of hot gals is your gold card.

Inside, your group fans out according to standard nightlife osmosis. As the night continues, you bump into each other, chat about the last 10 fantastic minutes, disappear, reappear. Then you see it. Behind the bar, glowing softly like a Celtic relic: a pristine bottle of Jameson.

You see it.

Ol' Jameson McJamie sees *you.*

He's alone. Brand-new. Untouched. In a brand-new bar. Someone, no, *you*, needs to set him free. You flag the bartender with a crisp $100 bill you paid $3.95 to extract from an ATM (terrible fiscal judgment). You order a double, neat, like a person who owns four cocktail books but doesn't know that "mixology" is Latin for *overpriced booze with most likely an egg white.*

It's poured. It's placed in your hand. You cheers some imaginary friend. Down the hatch.

Green light.

You immediately begin roaming the bar telling your friends you love them *so much.* You're floating. You're adored. You're invincible. You own this town. You order another. Journey comes on. You play air guitar. You fist-pump.

Total dork.

Zero shame.

Five hours later, you're still standing in the same general area. Your friends have come and gone. You're $185 deep. McJamie is over half empty. The original eight friends are now four. Then two. It's 1:45 a.m. The lights come on. Your air guitar has lost three strings.

You and two survivors stumble into the limo, utterly wiped. Thirty minutes back to the hotel.

This is where you wish you'd saved some elastic energy.

Elastic energy, by definition, is reversibility. Stretch. Snap back. No permanent damage. Sometimes. You nap in the limo. You're still buzzed but mobile, floating in that dangerous limbo where you think you're *exactly fine.* At the hotel, your friends beg you *173 times* to stay. You respond with *173 excuses* explaining why you're totally good to drive home.

Whatever. You've committed. You step into the dimly lit parking lot and start looking for your car.

Three minutes pass.

Four.

Nothing.

You laugh. Naturally, your car has been stolen. Of course it has.

Marching back to the front desk, you channel every *Law & Order* episode you've ever half-watched. You demand footage. You demand the police. You threaten to sue the hotel into bankruptcy.

"How could you people that work here LET my car get stolen?"

Fourteen minutes after terrorizing a poor overnight clerk who barely speaks English, you announce, while dramatically waving a cigarette in the air, that you'll wait *outside* for the cops to arrive after 2:41 a.m.

You exit the revolving doors, turn the corner to be respectful while lighting up another smoke, and—

There it is.

Your car. That red Dodge Daytona looking good!

Just… sitting there.

It's a Miracle.

You squint. Scrunch your face. Didn't you park on the *other* side of the hotel? Near the gas station?

No matter. The universe has smiled upon you.

You grab your keys from your purse, unlock that bitch, and drive off into the night.

Now elastic energy.

Twenty minutes later, red and blue lights.

You've been pulled over for driving the *exact car* you reported stolen an hour earlier.

Also—you're drunk.

Allostatic load of energy time.

Allostatic Load

Allostatic load is "the wear and tear on the body" which accumulates as an individual is exposed to repeated or chronic stress. The term was coined in 1993 by researchers Bruce McEwen and Eliot Stellar. It describes the physiological consequences of prolonged exposure to heightened neural and neuroendocrine stress responses. Jail helps you reset your allostatic load.

Understanding allostatic load is essential in your quest to quit drinking. A core function of the brain's regulatory systems is reducing uncertainty. Humans are wired to resist unpredictability. As a result, we constantly attempt to reduce uncertainty about future outcomes. Allostasis supports this by anticipating needs and preparing the body to meet them. This process consumes significant mental energy. When uncertainty remains unresolved, stress becomes chronic and allostatic load accumulates.

This brings us to Type 2 allostatic load.

Type 2 allostatic load occurs when ongoing energy demands consistently exceed available resources. It is driven by psychosocial pressures such as low socioeconomic status, major life events, and environmental instability. This helps explain the increased risk of cardiovascular disease and chronic conditions such as alcoholism, obesity, diabetes, hypertension, and severe mental illness among individuals exposed to trauma and social disadvantages.

Social and cultural systems often amplify this burden by perpetuating disparities in access to quality healthcare. Access to treatment for alcohol use is a clear example. Wealthier individuals can often afford more comprehensive treatment programs paid for out of pocket. Individuals with fewer financial resources face increasingly limited options as income decreases

When stress overwhelms an individual's ability to cope and becomes persistent, the result is allostatic load.

Contributing factors to allostatic load include the following: continual physiological arousal due to chronic stress, inadequate coping mechanisms, stress response continuing past the completion of a stressor, and an insufficient allostatic response to a stressor.

Under normal conditions, a stress response activates during a challenge and shuts off once the stressor ends. Allostatic load is the accumulation of stressors and maladaptive responses that may result in an extreme state, where the stress response does not terminate.

In simple terms, stress builds, and drinking becomes the coping mechanism.

Allostatic load affects both cognitive and physical functioning, particularly in the prefrontal cortex, hippocampus, and amygdala. If these terms are unfamiliar, further reading will deepen your understanding.

So how do we reduce or manage allostatic load? There are effective strategies.

Allostatic load differs by sex, age, and the social status of an individual. Protective factors can be introduced at different life stages to reduce stress and prevent excessive allostatic load. These factors include parental bonding, education, social support, healthy workplaces, a sense of meaning in one's choices, and generally positive emotional states. Eliminating alcohol is a foundational step that will create ripple effects across many areas of your life.

Personal interventions of various magnitudes can include encouraging sleep quality and quantity, social support, self-esteem and wellbeing, improving diet, avoiding alcohol or drug consumption, and participating in physical activity.

Providing cleaner and safer environments and the incentive towards a higher education of things will reduce the chance of stress and improve mental health significantly, therefore, reducing the onset of high allostatic load.

Please reread the entire above passage about allostatic energy and do further research on it as well. It is a critical component of sustained sobriety and can serve as the foundation for long-term recovery and life rebuilding. It is a keystone concept. Even people who do not drink can benefit from understanding this framework.

Edit Your Code (Allostatic Load Edition)

Quitting drinking is difficult because drinking is rarely the core problem. It is often the body's attempt to manage stress that has exceeded its capacity. Accumulated stress, whether mental, emotional, or physiological, is known as allostatic load.

Your mind and body are constantly trying to predict, adapt, and survive. To do that, they run an internal operating system built in real time. Parents, teachers, friends, culture, religion, politics, media, music, news, and the internet all write code into that system. Over time, repeated stressors force the system to work harder and harder to maintain balance.

Alcohol becomes a shortcut. It temporarily reduces perceived stress but at the cost of increasing allostatic load later.

If you don't regularly filter, test, and edit this internal code, it will default to whatever provides the fastest relief. That relief often comes with long-term damage.

Editing your code is not self-sabotage. It is load management. Early on, this may feel intense, almost disruptive, but that is the point. You are reducing chronic stress by changing the inputs, not white-knuckling the outputs.

The strategies that follow are not willpower tricks. They are allostatic load interventions.

Set Clear Goals (Reduce Uncertainty)

Uncertainty is one of the fastest ways to spike allostatic load. Clear, achievable goals lower it.

Start small. Commit to one sober week or month. Set limits you can realistically maintain. Stop assuming this should be easy, difficulty does not mean failure; it means your system is recalibrating. Being sober isn't convenient.

Remove Temptations (Lower Baseline Stress)

Constant exposure to alcohol keeps your nervous system on alert. That vigilance costs energy.

Remove alcohol from your home. Avoid high-risk environments early on. Change routines, like grocery routes, to reduce exposure. These small environmental changes significantly reduce load over time. Eventually, restraint becomes neutrality.

Find Alternative Activities (Restore Balance)

Alcohol often fills empty space created by fatigue, boredom, or emotional depletion.

Replace it with activities that restore rather than stimulate, such as movement, creative work, reading, gardening, or time with people who calm rather than drain you. If you have kids, shared activities are one of the most effective load reducers available.

Stay Hydrated (Support Physiological Regulation)

Dehydration increases stress hormones. Water supports regulation. Drink freely. For now, anything non-alcoholic is acceptable. Avoid NA beers early—they can reinforce the same neural loops. For many people, holding a water bottle satisfies the physical ritual without triggering the chemical cascade.

Practice Mindfulness (Interrupt Stress Loops)

Mindfulness is not spiritual fluff; it is nervous system hygiene. Short pauses—three minutes, ten breaths, quiet sitting—reduce cortisol and prevent escalation. Awareness without reaction lowers load. Engine off.

Seek Support (Distribute Load)

Humans are not designed to regulate stress alone. Friends, family, peers, therapists, and support groups distribute emotional weight. Some people need frequent check-ins; others need quiet accountability. Know yourself. Ask. Most people are willing to help. Avoid social media where possible.

Use Distraction Strategically (Delay Impulse)

Cravings peak and pass. You don't need to defeat them, only outlast them.

Redirect attention fully: walk with intention, clean something thoroughly, cook, listen deeply to music, or call someone who grounds you. Attention shifts reduce load by preventing rumination.

Reward Yourself (Replace Chemical Relief)

Alcohol often functions as the reward for surviving the day. Replace it intentionally. Choose rewards that require effort such as massages, experiences, planned outings. The more delayed and deliberate the reward, the stronger the neural rewiring.

Educate Yourself (Increase Predictability)

Knowledge reduces uncertainty, which reduces load. Learn what alcohol actually does to stress systems. Redirect curiosity into new domains. Ask your kids or friends to teach you something. Learning restores agency.

Take It One Day at a Time (Prevent Overload)

Allostatic load accumulates when future stress is anticipated too far ahead. Stay present. Win today. Setbacks are not system failures, they are data. Adjust and continue.

The Irish Mafia wants you regulated, not perfect. Olympic champions don't win every day; they show up every day. Airplanes didn't fly on the first attempt, but they eventually stayed airborne.

Both feet in.

Load down.

System rebuilding.

Now that we have thoroughly analyzed five whys, roadblocks, alternates, your personal energy stack and how allostatic loads are all critical elements to sober, we will unlock what should happen as you put these tools into practice investing in yourself. Moving forward.

3. Invest in Yourself: RFM.

RFM (Recency, Frequency, Monetization) is a framework used to analyze human behavior through three core metrics. Let's look at the specific definitions first, then apply them to drinking.

Remember bad money drives out good money. This is a principle based on Gresham's law and stretches back even to the end of the 5th century. Your face value of drinking is possibly perceived today just as valuable as tomorrow, when in reality, it is diminishing your life, driving out the good money, the good value. Unlock your intrinsic value hiding within your sober self. Alcohol devalues you. The good and bad money cannot circulate together. Do not let the vulgar displace the beauty. Let us help you invest in yourself.

Recency

Recency refers to how recently a person engaged in a specific behavior. In this context, it asks how recently you consumed alcohol. From a marketing perspective, someone who buys alcohol frequently and recently is considered a high-value customer. How recent was your last drink—today, yesterday, last month at a birthday? Journaling can help you track recency, especially if your drinking is sporadic. For many high-use drinkers, recency is nearly always daily. You should be reading this book sober. If you are not sober right now, put it down, take a shower, and do not pick it back up until you are. Read it sober.

Frequency

Frequency measures how often a behavior occurs within a given period. Applied to alcohol, frequency tracks how often you drink. Remember, sobriety is you versus you, not you versus anyone else. There are highly functioning drinkers who can mix vodka with anything, all day, and there are folks who just do the NFL Sunday beers, but cannot handle that. What matters here is frequency.

Monetization

Monetization measures how much money you spend on alcohol. For this analysis, focus primarily on alcohol itself, not the secondary costs around it. Track how much you actually spend on alcohol. Heavy spenders are considered high-value targets and are marketed to more aggressively. As you spend, they increase the marketing and you end up in a spiral or death loop.

Reducing recency, frequency, and monetization is not deprivation, it is reinvestment in yourself.

Now, let's apply RFM analysis with greater emphasis on the habits of alcohol consumption.

Recency

Knowing when you last bought or used alcohol reveals your current level of attachment to it. From a marketing standpoint, recent use makes you more receptive to ads, promotions, and social cues tied to drinking. That messaging is constant, oftentimes subliminal, and designed to keep your allostatic load high.

Now you're aware of it. The coincidental notification effect is part of the same system. As concern about your drinking increases, so does your awareness of alcohol-related messaging. It was always there, operating quietly in the background. Awareness simply brings it into focus.

Once a topic enters your conscious awareness, it naturally moves to the front of your mind. That awareness is not a weakness, it's the first interruption of an automatic stress-response cycle.

From an allostatic perspective, recency matters because the shorter the gap between drinks, the less time your nervous system has to return to baseline. Frequent recency keeps your stress-response machinery switched on.

Frequency

Tracking how often you drink exposes patterns and shows where intervention is possible. Daily drinkers require a different approach than weekend or social drinkers, but the comparison ends there. This is you versus you.

The time of day doesn't matter. It doesn't matter if it's 8 a.m., 5 p.m., or Sunday afternoon darts league. What matters is how often your system is activated by alcohol.

High frequency keeps your body locked in a heightened state of arousal. Reducing frequency gives your nervous system room to recover. Even small reductions lower allostatic load.

Breaking frequency into smaller segments makes reduction and eventual elimination more achievable. Some lifestyle reframing may feel forced at first, others will come naturally. Intentional or imperfect, action still counts. A downward trend is great. The trend is your friend.

Here are some basic ideas on reducing consumption.

The Sweetness of Nothing

Interrupt a habitual drinking time by replacing it with nothing. No drink, activity or heavy thoughts at all. Break the loop. Practice enjoying the moment without drinking or thinking about drinking and move to light thoughts.

Think of this as a mini allostatic reset. Sit quietly. Slow your breathing. Let your nervous system stand down. Rest your eyes. Do nothing on purpose. This is not inactivity—it's recovery.

Make Haste, Slowly

Take small, measured steps instead of large, dramatic leaps. Pour less. Use a smaller glass. Take the same amount of time to drink a smaller portion. Frequency may stay the same initially, but total load decreases.

Small wins stack. A beach isn't one grain of sand, it's

thousands adding up. Set micro-goals and reward consistency. This lowers stress without triggering rebound behavior.

Go for a Walk

Breaking frequency requires replacement activities. Walking is one of the simplest and most effective. Walk anywhere outside, inside, around the block, or in circles if needed.

Walking lowers cortisol, regulates breathing, and gives your brain something rhythmic and predictable to process. Notice sounds, movement, weather, people. Let your thoughts ebb and flow. This is an active way to unload stress.

The Wolf

Every endeavor has a wolf. Unexpected triggers. They will appear. Knowing this ahead of time shifts you from surprise to preparation. Someone brings wine at 11 a.m.? That's not a crisis, it's a test. Let them drink. You eat the cheese. No one is forcing anything. Reframe the obstacle, prepare, choose deliberately, and move on.

Prepared beats surprised every time. Visualization reduces stress load before it accumulates.

Age Is Just a Number

Frequency must be examined, adjusted, and recalibrated repeatedly. Starting at 25 looks different than starting at 55. That doesn't matter. Start anyway.

You are never too old to lower stress, reclaim recovery cycles, and rebuild capacity. The right time is now.

Make It Effortless

Where possible, cultivate ease. Ease lowers allostatic demand. Quiet confidence builds momentum without friction.

Others may not understand your progress. That's fine. Keep moving. Practice ease until it becomes natural. When effort drops, sustainability rises.

Life Is Beautiful

As frequency decreases, notice what you gain: clarity, time, presence, health. Journal it. Progress won't always feel euphoric. Sometimes it looks like coffee instead of wine. A sunset without a glass in the way. Genuine laughter with people who matter most. These moments regulate your nervous system more than alcohol ever did.

No one savors the moment they're vomiting a burrito onto the bathroom floor at 9:45 p.m. Reduction replaces chaos with dignity.

Monetization

Money matters, both financial and social. Social currency is harder to earn and far more valuable. Reducing alcohol spending creates immediate surplus. This is found money. Less spending reduces stress, which lowers allostatic load further. It compounds.

Monetization is about where money goes. Budgeting is about controlling it. By removing alcohol, you reverse the flow: instead of funding stress, you reclaim resources.

Let's flip the model. Instead of habits extracting value from you, start extracting value by breaking them.

Time to do a budget exercise.

Budget Exercise: Know What You're Really Spending

If you want to cut back or quit drinking, understanding your **real cost** is a game-changer. Not just booze, but all the collateral damage that keeps your nervous system stuck in stress-mode. This is how you budget it, calculate it, and stare that allostatic load right in the eyeballs. Read the rest of the chapter, then come back and really think about this exercise.

Step 1 — Alcohol Only

How much do you spend on alcohol each month?
This is straight booze — nothing else.

Alcohol spend: $_______________________

Step 2 — Activity Costs

Now consider where you drink. If you go to your local shithole for trivia, hit the golf course and sip your way through 18 holes, fish with a six-pack at your side, or hit any other booze-related activity, **add all associated costs** here. Include fees, food, tickets, drinks other than booze (yeah, that matters), and any props.

Expenses may include but are not limited to:

- Trivia entry fees
- Green fees on the golf course / Fishing licenses or bait
- Dinner
- Cover charges/ entry charge / taxi to and fro, yo!

Activity costs: $_______________________

Step 3 — The Extras

What else do you do when you drink? Smoke pot? Puff a cigar like a mob boss? Play the slots? Tip like you're the Lord Mayor of Liquid Courage? Buy rounds you don't drink? Late night tacos? **Add it all.**

Extras: $_____________________

Step 4 — Time Is Money

Time is stress load and opportunity cost. Calculate the **total hours** you spend in these environments per month. Then multiply by your average hourly wage — regardless of whether it's on your day off.

Hours spent: _______________
Hourly wage: _______________
Time cost (hours × wage): $_________________________

Step 5 — Optional (but Realistic) Risk

You *might* think a DUI won't happen to you. The Irish Mafia says:
You think it won't… until it does.

Budget a conservative estimate for legal trouble, insurance hikes, fines, and lost time.

Say $200 a month.

Risk buffer: $200

✔ Monthly Drinking Budget Worksheet

1. Alcohol only: $_______________________
2. Activity costs: $_______________________
3. Extras: $_______________________
4. Time cost: $_______________________
5. Risk buffer: $200

Total Monthly Drinking Budget: $_______________________

This is what you are actually "budgeting" on drinking — not the fantasy number you tell yourself. This number reflects **stress, time, money, risk, and opportunity cost** all wrapped into one ugly truth.

Why This Matters (Irish Mafia Perspective)

You think the cost of a drink is $9? That's a joke. That's the headline number, the line item in the bar tab. The **deeper cost** is what keeps your stress systems jammed in high gear.

Every dollar you drop feeds the cycle:

- Recency keeps you in the queue, exposed to cues and cravings
- Frequency keeps your nervous system in a chronic stress loop
- Monetization funds the very behaviors that spike allostatic load

The more you spend, the more marketing and social cues press you to spend again. It's a feedback loop. It's engineered. It's the economic equivalent of drinking to self-soothe a body already overloaded. Your job now is to **pull that cycle apart** and redirect every dollar, and every hour, back into your life.

MONETIZATION

Now let's talk about monetization. This is the part everyone avoids and the part that actually runs the show.

You already calculated how many hours you spend drinking: trivia night, boys' night out, the local shithole, and golfing. You also totaled the direct costs. Together, that number represents how much you must earn, after taxes, just to maintain the activity of drinking.

Yes, golf and fishing are fun. And darts is apparently a sport somewhere on ESPN. We get it. These activities get labeled "stress relief." We're not telling you to stop doing them. Just hang on.

Money isn't earned only at work. There's also social currency that is often ignored because it doesn't come with a dollar sign, even though it carries enormous value. When you reduce or quit drinking, you reclaim real money and unlock social currency at the same time.

You may already be rationalizing: cocktails with clients build relationships. Alcohol hasn't slowed your progress. Everything feels normal to you. That's the problem. Your perception becomes your reality, but it is not shared by the room. Other people do not see you the way you see yourself. People see what you appear to be, few experience what you really are.

When you reduce or stop drinking, the equity of your social currency improves immediately. If you quit for one month, you save the money, obviously. Less obvious: your social standing improves unless you turn into a complete jackass, which is unlikely.

You'll probably do those drinking-centered activities less. That's not a loss. That's replacement theory taking hold.

Replacement theory is simple: you remove one behavior and replace it with another. Same activity, different version, or a completely new one. The alcohol version no longer serves you, so it gets swapped out. This is how change actually sticks.

Now you have options. Save the money or redeploy it. If imagination isn't firing, here's a short list:

- Invest. Compounding works whether you believe in it or not.
- Pay down debt. Less debt equals less stress. Period.
- Travel. Culture beats bar stools. Perspective beats hangovers.
- Build an emergency fund. Alcohol-related emergencies are optional—avoid them.
- Movement. Small fitness goals beat big plans that never start.
- Pick a hobby that requires attention. Engagement replaces consumption.
- Learn something new. Curiosity compounds faster than alcohol ever did.
- Improve your space. Better environments produce better thinking. Think Feng Shui or decluttering.
- Give back. Contribution builds purpose. Purpose lowers stress.
- Spend quality time. Memories outlast money. This is the highest return.

Get out of the bar.

As drinking fades, social currency compounds quietly. You feel better. You look better. You sleep better. You're still going to think about alcohol, that's normal. You notice the thought and move on.

We're not therapists, but we know this: irritable people repel others. That's universal.

When you're sober, your value to others increases. Trust rises. People share more. Vulnerability shows up. That's real currency. If someone doesn't value the sober version of you, that's their problem—not yours.

Earn your social currency. Bank it.

The Irish Mafia doesn't chase coins, we compound value. Don't let good money drive out bad.

The Irish Mafia's Final Word on Budgeting

Cutting back isn't about austerity. It's about **regaining autonomy** over your body, your time, your nervous system, and your wallet.

You did not get here by accident. You got here because your brain learned that alcohol reduces stress *in the moment* even while it spikes stress over the long run. That's an allostatic load. And it's reversible.

This worksheet isn't just numbers on a page. It's a **mirror**. It's the truth you've been ignoring. It's the first step in taking back your nervous system from the relentless marketing, the social triggers, the "harmless fun," and the allostatic wreckage that comes with it.

Fill it in sober, look at it sober, and then start cutting those numbers down, one real dollar at a time. You're not budgeting for booze anymore. You're budgeting for **freedom**.

Now we will embark on the concept of social currency and what it means for you today and going forward. If you are unaware of your social currency today, read about it, then think about it. You have social currency. You just need to figure out if your bank balance is positive or negative and what your proverbial social credit score is.

The Irish Mafia Code of Social Currency

A Short Doctrine. You are a brand. You may not have chosen it, but you own it. Every action you take either deposits into or withdraws from your social currency. There is no neutral. Currency compounds or it collapses.

1. Trust Is the Only Real Asset

Trust and credibility are the foundation. Without them, nothing trades. Say what you will do, then do it. Start small. Execute cleanly. Stack wins. Rome wasn't built in a day, and neither is a reputation, but it can burn down overnight.

Do not overpromise. Do not volunteer for things you can't deliver. If you don't know how to do something, connect the person to someone who does. Connectors compound value. Liabilities destroy it.

2. Protect the Brand at All Costs

Your behavior is always being observed, especially when you think it isn't. Showing up hungover, being the first to drink at work events, ordering shots no one asked for, yelling in bars. All of these moves drain social currency fast when the wrong eyes are watching.

You never truly know how you look through other people's eyes. Assume the version they see is less flattering than the one in your head. Act accordingly.

Being "the life of the party" doesn't require alcohol. Being sober doesn't mean being dull, it means being precise. If you need guardrails, get a code word from someone you trust and listen when they use it. We suggest the word pineapple.

3. Reciprocity Builds Power

Social currency grows through reciprocity. Who can you count on? Who counts on you? You don't need to give back immediately, but you must intend to. When you do give back, do it cleanly and without scoreboard-keeping.

Early sobriety requires borrowing strength. That's not weakness, that's strategy. Pay it forward later.

4. Depth Beats Size

Your network's depth matters more than its size. A few solid allies beat a room full of drunks every time. Ignore the fringe. Focus on the people closest to you. These are the ones who open doors, vouch for you, and tell the truth when it matters.

Ask good questions. Listen more than you speak. Be present. Awareness of others is power, so long as you mind your own business.

5. Control the Stress Load

Alcohol inflates allostatic load. It borrows relief today and charges interest tomorrow. When you remove alcohol, stress doesn't vanish, it redistributes. Your job is to lower the baseline.

Sleep. Move your body. Reduce chaos. Replace bar hours with quieter, stabilizing rituals. Walks beat hangovers. Calm beats bravado. Lower load equals higher performance.

6. Build Quiet Momentum

Move deliberately. Avoid overcorrection. Ease compounds faster than force. Quiet confidence feeds itself. Let results speak before words do If an opportunity advances your life with minimal cost, research it. If it aligns, engage. Be selective. Find your lane. Build expertise. Leverage it.

7. Bank the Currency

Social currency is a store of value. It buys trust, access, patience, and forgiveness. Sober currency trades at a higher rate. People are willing to share vulnerability with someone who is present, clear, and steady.

If others don't value the sober version of you, that's their problem, not yours. Your self-induced value is what matters. This is your journey.

Earn your social currency.

Protect it.

Bank it.

Investing in Yourself: Age Brackets and Whys Behind Drinking

Pause. We will now review, by age bracket, reasons for drinking, and begin setting new patterns. Get honest. If you drink, you've been doing it long enough for it to feel normal. If you're 21, you're early and that's good. If you're 72, you're not late, also good. Starting today still counts. Let's stop giving alcohol days it hasn't earned.

Your reasons for drinking change with age. Your strategy should too. Use the following bracket that fits you, circle what hits, and ignore the rest. This isn't astrology—it's pattern recognition.

Ages 21–30: Access, Identity, Gravity

At this age, drinking is driven by availability, boredom, and the need to belong.

Turning 21 makes alcohol legal. If you started earlier, the milestone already flattened. There is no balloon pop, it's just a habit. College and young-adult culture often treat drinking like the entry fee. Add boredom and FOMO and suddenly it feels mandatory.

Patterns reproduce. You see something enough times, you call it normal, then you copy it—how people dress, talk, celebrate, and drink. Look around. Which patterns are yours, and which ones did you borrow?

Peer pressure here is identity pressure. Friends are building their image and want you as a supporting character. Ironically, abstaining is the power move but most people your age can't see it yet.

The birthdays stack fast. Endless 21sts. A plan exists. Decline without explaining. "I'm not drinking tonight" is a complete sentence.

Curiosity is real. So is the cost. The same story on loop of doing shots, dumb decisions, blackout, repeat, gets old fast. The shine wears off. The bank account drops. Decide early what you're willing to pay.

Stress shows up too. School, money, work, relationships. Alcohol pretends to help, then steals coping skills.

Exercise: write down what alcohol has already taken—time, money, mornings, focus. Then write what you want back. That list matters.

Music, movies, influencers, and ads don't sell moderation. They sell identity.

Family patterns matter. You can break them only if you stop pretending they aren't there.

Ages 30–40: Load, Pressure, Justification

This decade is heavy. Careers, partners, kids, expectations. Drinking becomes "earned" or "deserved."

Work events and dinners push alcohol as social glue. Bring your own non-alcoholic option if needed so you're not stuck with tap water and commentary.

Stress is real. Deadlines, burnout, money pressure. Cutting alcohol often lowers baseline stress, unless your environment is toxic. If it is, change the environment, not just the drink.

Parenthood exposes everything. If you're drinking to survive bedtime, that's not "wine time," that's a coping gap. Alcohol doesn't raise your kids, you do. But it will if you let it.

Quick reflection: pick one year between ages 5–15. How many family events had alcohol in the background? That's how "normal" installs itself. Decide what your kids will remember.

Transitions such as marriage, divorce, babies, moving domiciles are all prime triggers. Build tools before drinking habits harden.

Dating with beer goggles is a terrible screening process. Try using your actual judgment. Burping on your date all night? Not good.

Ages 50–60: Routine, Identity, Inertia

Here, drinking often hides in routine.

Work stress, caregiving, money worries. The alcohol masquerades as relief, then quietly adds weight to the load called life. Events such as retirement, empty nest, divorce, loss can spike drinking or restart it. You are not at the end of the line. You're at a pivot. Relapse might lurk around the corner like Jack the Ripper. Be strong.

Reclaim curiosity. Act like a curious 20-year-old again. Start new routines, new learning, new discomfort. Curiosity beats stagnation. Ask yourself what your 80 year old self would tell you now! Habits don't retire when you do. They follow you home. New ones form faster than you think if you stop defending the old ones.

If your friends can't handle you drinking less, upgrade your circle. Friends advise. Peers pressure. Know the difference.

Ages 70+: Choice, Connection, Clarity

Some drink less with age. Others drink from grief, pain, isolation, or boredom. This stage can be peak happiness if you protect your health and relationships.

Common drivers: habit, loneliness, loss, depression, pain, boredom, and ignorance of medication interactions.

Alcohol hits harder and lingers longer now. If it's affecting balance, memory, or continence, talk to a doctor. That's not weakness, that's you being intelligent.

Replace isolation with connection. Join something. Volunteer. Learn. Even people-watching counts as an activity. Just don't narrate out loud what you see to strangers sitting next to you, or it's 5150 time.

Boredom at Any Age

Boredom isn't harmless. Many times it's often the real problem. If you drink out of boredom, find a bigger problem. Learn something hard. Build something. Train for something. Mentor. Serve. Alcohol thrives in empty space.

Zoom-out exercise: right now, from a satellite view, strangers don't matter. Zoom back in—your spouse, kids, parents, and closest allies do. Reduce drinking for the people who live with the version of you that shows up every day.

Underage Drinking (If This Applies)

Underage drinking carries irreversible risks, including brain development, accidents, legal fallout, lives destroyed in one night. If this is you or someone you love, get help early. "Everyone does it" isn't a defense when consequences arrive.

At any age, spotting patterns means you're already winning. Once patterns are visible, the problem stops being mysterious and starts being manageable.

The Irish Mafia rule still stands: small daily wins beat heroic promises. Stack them. Guard your energy. Earn your next version deliberately. Keep the voltage high and energy up.

Build Your New Pattern

- Set no more than three Golden Goals
- Apply disciplined focus
- Clarify short-term targets
- Define long-term outcomes
- Write your code: a mission statement that governs action and replaces old habits

Not drinking is a journey. On a difficulty scale of 1–10, with 10 being the most direct and demanding path to sobriety, there are many ways forward. A 10 is teleportation: a full, immediate stop. From there, the scale slides down to a 1, whatever your personal starting point may be. Your 1 might be skipping Monday drinks or staying sober at the next birthday. It's your journey, and like any worthwhile one, it will have twists and turns. Your journey might feel like planning a trip to the moon with only enough fuel to reach the corner store.

Let's talk about patterns. Many coaches and thinkers talk about how patterns are built, reinforced, and broken. This next section draws influence from Napoleon Hill, whose ideas apply well beyond alcohol. While we're using drinking as the lens, patterns shape every part of life.

Talk to anyone about their routines and you'll see how much of life unfortunately runs on autopilot.

Most people repeat the same motions day after day. Faces and places change, but the pattern stays intact. Think about your drive to work, your evenings, your bedtime routine. That's where alcohol quietly inserts itself. What do you give up to make room for a drink?

Quiet routines slowly mold you into something you never chose to be. This is your prison. Before you break a pattern, you have to see it for what it is: a structure built from repetition, comfort, and fear of the unknown. If you don't recognize the problem, you'll never try to escape it. No one will hand you this awareness, you have to claim it.

Are you living, or just surviving in a loop? Many drinking patterns are inherited, learned, normalized by culture or family, or reinforced by past versions of yourself. Familiarity doesn't mean healthy. Recognition is the first step. You stop running on autopilot and start asking better questions.

Fear disguises itself as logic. Self-doubt wears humility like a costume. Years of postponing change quietly become your identity.

What would change if you stopped today? Procrastination only delays awareness and awareness stings. But that sting is the doorway to change. You cannot escape a prison you won't admit you're in.

Humans are meant to grow, adapt, and evolve. Your script isn't written by outside forces, it's written by you. It's time to flip the switch. Break the rhythm without burning your life down. Try a new responsibility, a new group, a new challenge. Be careful not to trade one dead pattern for another. Growth should elevate your purpose.

You are the 1%. Staying asleep is easier. Change is uncomfortable, painful, and uncertain, but that's the cost of freedom.

Comfort is a seductive liar. It tells you you're fine when you're stuck. Daily, you must earn the right to rest.

This isn't peace or progress, it's a cage disguised as a reward. Drinking erodes your edge until you forget who you were becoming. Lean into discomfort. Attend the dinner and don't drink. Do it again. That's evolution. Don't chase security; build strength. Time doesn't belong to you, you belong to time. Start today.

Pain isn't your enemy; it's your compass. Most people avoid it, numb it, or outrun it. That's a mistake. Pain shows you exactly what needs to change. The 1% doesn't wait to be cornered by divorce, jail, or tragedy. They choose pressure early. Every transformation starts with a snapping point. Harness that moment. Say enough. Some people stay in pain and build their lives around it. Others use it as fuel. If people fall away, that's not betrayal, it's your evolution.

Sobriety should sharpen you, not harden you. Pain leads to destruction or rebirth. That choice is yours. Forget blind positivity when what you need is a blueprint. You don't paint over cracks; you rebuild the foundation. You don't need a revolution, just a spark. One small shift, repeated with intention. Journal. Change how you wake up. Change what you say before entering a room. Blueprints begin with a single line.

Motivation is unreliable. Momentum matters. Discipline wins. Try one new thing today. Interrupt the pattern. Move a fraction outside your routine. Small steps stack. You are proving the pattern isn't stronger than you.

Discipline isn't about perfection, it's about showing up again. One sober day is easy. Hundreds of imperfect days are the work. Broken self-promises kill trust. Keep one promise. Stack another. Discipline becomes identity.

Breaking patterns is only half the fight. Freedom without direction leads to relapse. Decide who you're becoming. Define your values. Build your new pattern with intention. Quitting alcohol is the direction and everything else follows. If you don't define your value, life will assign it. Build something that pulls you forward. This is your blueprint. Play to win.

In developing your set of **Golden Goals & Patterns** to successfully move forward, we present the large concept of 'Game Theory' as explained in the context of alcohol & substance abuse and the subsequent reduction or elimination of usage. This is a robust approach of 'playing to win' at sobriety and also used in many business decision making processes.

The Art of Sober uses Game Theory to become sober. Bet on yourself and win.

Game Theory and Alternatives

Game theory is a mathematical framework used to analyze decision-making when multiple individuals or entities interact and each person's choices affect the outcome for others. It is commonly used in economics, political science, biology, and other fields to understand strategic behavior and predict outcomes.

Here, we apply it to quitting drinking: you versus the booze.

In the context of reducing or eliminating alcohol use, game theory offers insight into your decision-making, your interactions with others, and strategies for lasting behavior change. It provides a way to think clearly about incentives, pressure, temptation, and support without turning sobriety into an emotional free-for-all.

Here's how game theory applies to your sober goals.

Incentive Design

Game theory can be used to design incentives that reduce alcohol use. By examining the costs and benefits of different choices you can create meaningful incentives that encourage healthier behavior.

Many of these incentives must be set by you, though others may emerge naturally. Life insurance applications, for example, directly assess alcohol consumption. So do job opportunities, relationships, health outcomes, and credibility. Incentives are already in play whether you acknowledge them or not.

Social Norms and Peer Pressure

Game theory helps explain how social norms and peer pressure influence drinking in environments like after-work happy hours, barbecues, weddings, or neighborhood events. Once you understand the environment you're entering, you can prepare accordingly.

Mentally run through the likely scenarios. Visualize what will happen at the Fourth of July barbecue. Picture the offers, the jokes, the pressure. Then decide in advance how you'll handle each one. Preparation turns surprise into strategy.

Treatment Compliance and Relapse Prevention

Game theory can model treatment compliance and relapse prevention by weighing the costs of relapse against the benefits of consistency and support. This helps you design personal strategies that improve long-term outcomes.

You might choose a structured plan or a looser one, formal treatment or peer support, online communities or in-person accountability. The structure matters less than your commitment to a system that works for you.

Self-Control and Temptation

Game theory sheds light on decision-making when temptation is present. Avoiding the alcohol aisle or skipping the beer tent at a local festival can significantly reduce cravings. Environmental control is not a weakness, it's a strategy.

If you've ever seen a car breathalyzer required after a DUI, that's the government applying game theory to influence behavior and outcomes. They employ it. So should you.

Pre-commitment, reminders, boundary-setting, and trigger avoidance are all practical applications of strategic thinking.

Cooperative Strategies and Peer Support

Game theory also explains why peer support works. Groups like AA are a classic example of cooperative strategy: shared goals, mutual accountability, and collective reinforcement.

Working with others increases the cost of failure and the reward of progress. Cooperation changes the game.

Intervention Planning

Game theory can also model interventions by simulating different outcomes and unintended consequences. Whether you're the one receiving help or offering it, understanding the complexity of interventions makes them more effective.

No matter your role, clarity beats chaos.

Choosing Your System

Before moving into goal setting, you may find game theory too complex or simply not your preferred framework. That's fine. Unless you live in the woods like a hermit or on a mountaintop like a monk, you interact with people, and any system that helps you navigate those interactions is worth considering.

The point is not the theory. The point is having a system.

A system provides the foundational blueprint from which you operate. How you frame and visualize your effort directly affects your results.

Consider this: reducing alcohol consumption is like piloting a plane. You need a steady hand on the controls, small course corrections, and awareness of turbulence. Alcohol is turbulence. Your WHY is the destination. Support systems are your co-pilots. You don't need to fly perfectly, you just need to stay on course.

There are alternative frameworks to game theory, and you may adopt one of them—or none at all. You may decide they're useless, or you may have a breakthrough. We are simply providing options. What matters is this: pick a system, commit to it, and move forward. You must move forward.

The following are some alternative theory systems.

Decision Theory

Decision theory examines how people make choices under uncertainty. Unlike game theory, which focuses on strategic interaction between people, decision theory puts the weight squarely on the individual. That means you. You choose. You own it.

Applied to drinking, decision theory forces clarity. You stop drifting and start deciding.

Identifying Goals

Decision theory demands that you define your goals clearly. Reduce drinking. Quit entirely. Or set firm boundaries. These are your goals, not a committee decision, not a family vote, not a social compromise. When goals are clear, decisions get easier.

Considering Risks and Uncertainty

Every choice carries risk. Continued drinking comes with known risks: health problems, legal exposure, financial damage, and relationship strain. Change carries uncertainty. Decision theory asks a simple question: which risk are you willing to live with? Known decay, or temporary discomfort?

Analyzing Costs and Benefits

This framework forces a brutal comparison. Short-term relief versus long-term consequences. Drinking might buy you a night of numbness. Sobriety buys you health, money, trust, and self-respect. Pick your return on investment.

Values and Trade-offs

Your values matter. If health, family, competence, or leadership rank higher than escape, your decisions must reflect that. Quick pleasure is expensive. Long-term damage is non-refundable.

Thresholds and Limits

Decision theory allows hard lines. Frequency caps. Quantity caps. Time-bound goals. A goal without a timeline is just a thought. Structure creates traction.

Monitor and Adjust

If you're deep into something that clearly isn't working, you have two choices: adjust or sabotage yourself by pressing forward. Ignoring feedback is how people stay stuck. Adjustment is how progress happens.

Decision theory works because it removes excuses. You are responsible. And that's power.

Social Exchange Theory

Social exchange theory says people act based on perceived costs and benefits in relationships. Drinking is often banked as a social currency but most people overestimate the value of business related drinking.

Ask yourself: what do you actually gain by drinking with your boss? With clients? With strangers at the bar? And what does it quietly cost you?

Costs vs. Benefits

Drinking may offer stress relief or social lubrication. It also delivers hangovers, missed opportunities, poorer judgment, and reputational erosion. No one plans to die early or implode their life, yet daily drinking quietly signals exactly that.

Alternatives

Most benefits alcohol claims to provide—connection, relaxation, belonging—are available elsewhere, with fewer consequences. Hobbies, fitness, skill-building, solitude, or real conversation outperform booze over time.

Social Support

Choose your exchanges wisely. The stranger at the bar has no stake in your future. The people who challenge your drinking do. Build exchanges that strengthen you, not ones that drain you.

Reinforcement

Reward progress. Take a day off. Book the massage. Cook the meal. Buy the thing. Reinforcement locks behavior in place. Celebrate wins or they fade. Bet on yourself, work on yourself, be yourself.

Social exchange theory reminds you: your environment shapes your behavior. Choose better trades.

Rational Choice Theory

Rational choice theory assumes people act to maximize benefit based on available information. When applied soberly, key word sober, it becomes obvious how bad alcohol is at math.

Cost–Benefit Reality

Make a real pros-and-cons list. Be honest. Alcohol rarely wins once emotion is stripped away.

Incentives and Deterrents

Better health. Stronger relationships. Clear mornings. Financial stability. These are incentives. DUIs, shame, lost trust, and stalled careers are deterrents. One list grows. The other doesn't.

Information Matters

Drunk decisions and sober decisions are not comparable. Same situation. Two outcomes. That alone should terrify you.

Risk Management

Short term: don't drive drunk seems logical. Long term: don't put yourself where bad decisions are likely. Rational people don't test guardrails at highway speed. Rational choice theory isn't moral. It's practical. It asks: does this move make sense?

Behavioral Economics Theory

Behavioral economics accepts that humans are biased, emotional, and imperfect. Instead of fighting that, it designs around it.

Nudges and Defaults

Make non-alcoholic options easier than alcohol. What's visible gets chosen. Stock your fridge accordingly.

Rewards and Framing

Reward progress immediately. Frame sobriety in gains, not losses: better sleep, sharper thinking, more money. Humans move toward reward faster than away from pain.

Commitment Devices

Contracts. Apps. Coins. Accountability partners. Tools work because willpower fluctuates. Systems don't. Get what you need sooner than later.

Bias Awareness

Present bias favors now over later. That's why milestones matter. One day. One week. One month. Stack them. Plan and achieve your goals.

Behavioral economics doesn't ask you to be perfect. It asks you to be smart about your flaws and idiosyncratic behaviors.

Evolutionary Game Theory

Some habits once served a purpose. They don't anymore. Alcohol may have bonded earlier generations. Today, it isolates, weakens, and dulls. That's an evolutionary mismatch. Old wiring in a new world. Recognize it. Update the strategy.

Choose bonding without poison. Stress relief without self-destruction. Cooperation without collapse. Adaptation is survival.

Network Theory

Your network determines your outcomes. Your social circle of trust. Surround yourself with like minded folks as much as you feel comfortable with.

Influence

Some people quietly push you toward drinking. Others don't. Choose proximity carefully.

Norms

If the group drinks, you drink. If the group trains, learns, or builds—you follow. Change the network or it will change you. Many would say you are in a drinking matrix, get out.

Support

Strong networks provide accountability and perspective. Weak networks provide noise and excuses.

Visualization

Map where your time goes. Most people discover they've been donating energy to people and places that return nothing.

Network theory makes it simple: who you're around is who you become.

Complexity Theory

This theory posits alcohol abuse isn't one problem. It's many systems tangled together—biology, stress, habit, environment, identity. Small changes matter. One brick doesn't build a wall. Stacked deliberately, they do. Don't let alcohol be a negative brick in the wall. Listen to that album and you can find countless subdued references to coping with addiction. Don't get fooled again. Shake it up. Interrupt feedback loops. Change routines. Replace environments. Adapt as you go. Resilience beats perfection. Progress beats purity.

Cooperative Game Theory

You don't have to do this alone. Coalitions work. One person or many. Shared goals create momentum. Accountability sharpens commitment. Bring others. Not to burden them, but to anchor yourself. Recovery isn't weakness. It's coordination.

Peer Counseling and Mentorship

Cooperative game theory works well with peer counseling and mentorship programs. They are powerful tools in recovery. People with lived experience bring credibility, clarity, and zero bullshit. They've been there. They know the traps, the excuses, and the shortcuts that don't work. That kind of guidance can't be faked.

Peer support networks create a place to share experiences, hard-earned insights, and real world tested coping strategies. Over time, this builds solidarity and camaraderie—the kind that says, *you're not alone, but you are responsible.*

Social Norms and Shared Expectations

Positive social norms inside supportive communities matter. When respect, empathy, and accountability are reinforced, not just talked about, people feel accepted without being coddled. That acceptance lowers stigma and removes barriers to asking for help.

Move past people who criticize your decision to reduce or stop drinking. Yes, cutting people off can feel hard until it doesn't. Once you weigh the costs and benefits, the reward becomes obvious. Fewer voices, more clarity. Less noise, more momentum.

The Art of Sober encourages disciplined analysis and decisive action. If someone threatens your progress, they're not part of your future. Period.

Applying cooperative game theory to recovery works because it mirrors real life: progress accelerates when people align around shared goals. Teamwork creates accountability, mutual support, and leverage. Barriers fall faster when you're not carrying the weight alone.

This kind of collective effort builds resilience and creates environments that actively support recovery, not just talk about it. Together, these forces strengthen long-term sobriety and well-being. Keep it small. Keep it tight. Build your circle like your life depends on it, because it does.

Final Word

These theories are not academic exercises. They are tools. Pick one. Use it. Build a system. Systems outlast motivation. You are creating your blueprint to build a new life.

You don't drift into sobriety. You engineer it. Move forward. Climbing a mountain is one foot in front of the other.

Golden Gains

Let us pause for a moment and take inventory. This framework isn't theory for theory's sake, it's leverage. It shows you exactly what you gain when alcohol is no longer running the show. These gains become your reminders, your anchors, and, eventually, your WHY. You don't need to romanticize sobriety. The benefits will show up.

Here's what starts happening when you stop drinking on real timelines, not motivational posters from social media.

24 Hours

Within the first 24 hours, your body begins correcting course.

Hydration

Alcohol drains fluids. Remove it, and your body immediately starts rebalancing. Better circulation. Better function. Less drag.

Sleep

Alcohol knocks you out but wrecks sleep architecture. Without it, sleep becomes deeper, quieter, and more restorative.

Liver Response

Your liver stops firefighting and starts repairing. Enzyme activity begins trending back toward normal.

Blood Sugar Stability

Alcohol spikes and crashes blood sugar. Remove it, and energy levels even out. Fewer dips. Less irritability.

Mental Clarity

The fog lifts. Focus improves. Decisions sharpen. You feel more present.

Inflammation Drops

Alcohol fuels systemic inflammation. Take it away, and the body calms down.

Mood Regulation

Neurotransmitters begin stabilizing. Anxiety softens. Irritability drops. Yes, including "being a jackass."

Calories & Weight

Alcohol is empty fuel. Cut it out, and weight loss often starts without trying.

Digestion

The gut stops getting irritated. Less bloating. Fewer emergencies.

Immune Function

Your immune system gets back on duty instead of playing catch-up.

Bottom line: 24 hours delivers real wins. Not miracles, but real momentum. And momentum matters.

25–48 Hours

Between 25–48 hours, recovery accelerates.

Hydration deepens. Inflammation continues to fall. Blood sugar stabilizes further, cutting cravings. Sleep improves again. You achieve longer REM cycles and fewer wake-ups. Liver repair continues. Neurotransmitters rebalance, improving mood and mental steadiness.

Digestion calms. Skin begins to rehydrate and brighten. Mental clarity sharpens—but hear this clearly: early sobriety can surface anger. That's not failure. That's awareness without anesthesia. Handle it. Don't aim it at civilians. As they say, least said, soonest mended. Don't get crazy and angry at people. If you do, realize hurt feelings are most quickly healed by not revisiting the event giving rise to the hurt. Don't blame alcohol, just learn and move on.

This is where sprint goals matter. Another 12 hours. Another night. Stack them.

72 Hours

At 49–72 hours, the early gains consolidate.

Hydration, sleep, digestion, blood sugar, liver function, mood stability, and mental clarity all continue improving. Hormones begin recalibrating, providing lower cortisol and better balance overall.

This is amplification. What you did in the first two days now compounds. Pair this with movement, reading, training, or structure, and the gains multiply.

30 Days+

Thirty days sober isn't a break—it's a pivot point.

People love Dry January and then walk right back into the fire. Why? Because they never defined what they were building toward. Sure, if you define a 30 day break, great. You achieved it. If you are looking to get sober, if you can do 30, you can do 15 more. Then another 15. Momentum is a choice.

At 30 days, the human body gains stack hard:

- Improved liver health
- Lower risk of heart disease, stroke, and cancer
- Reduced blood pressure and inflammation
- Better sleep, digestion, mood stability, and mental clarity
- Stronger immune response
- Noticeably better hygiene and self-care (yes, people notice)

This is where habits stop feeling forced and start feeling normal. Your position size of intrinsic value increases dramatically.

Results vary based on genetics, lifestyle, and health—but the direction is universal. Less alcohol equals more capacity, more liquidity.

You're not chasing perfection. You're building leverage. One day at a time. Sometimes one hour at a time. Each block stacks on the last. Keep moving. You are no longer living in the idiosyncratic bubble.

Engineering Yours Sober Blueprint

At The Art of Sober, we value practical understanding. When new ideas connect to things you already recognize, they become easier to grasp, apply, and sustain. This usually leads to better outcomes. Give thought to the pathway options, and remember you are allowed to change at any time. This framework is meant to get you grounded and started.

In this section, we focus on goal pathways that are not buried in abstract philosophical ramblings or academic jargon that require advanced degrees or therapist jargon to decode. We keep it clear and usable—easy to review, assess, and apply—so you can choose a structured blueprint that moves you forward with your sobriety and recovery journey. By aligning with natural transformation occurrences in the world, one can better identify with a method and emulate that in their recovery journey.

Editor's note: You will see the word "reduced" used alongside "abstain" in this section, and that is intentional. Not everyone quits cold turkey on day one, and some people simply need to rein in their consumption. The following framework is designed for everyone, not only those who require complete abstinence. We all have different goals, and while optimism is useful, realism is required if you want results.

To reiterate, to ground the sober journey in something memorable, we're going to use an animal metaphor. You may have heard the term "spirit animal," or you may not have. You don't need to overcommit to the idea. Simply choose one of the animal transformations whose traits resonate with you and then begin to live by those traits.

Let's begin with several transformation-based concepts that apply to reducing or abstaining from alcohol.

Hibernation

In this context, hibernation means taking a deliberate break from drinking. Just as animals hibernate to conserve energy, you can pause alcohol for a defined window—two weeks, a month, whatever is realistic—to reassess your habits and experience the benefits of sobriety without overthinking the whole future at once.

Animals commonly associated with hibernation include bears, hedgehogs, ground squirrels, bats, and certain reptiles and amphibians. The point isn't biology trivia. The point is the strategy: conserve energy, reduce stress, and come out clearer.

Chrysalis

A chrysalis transformation represents deep internal change and growth. The kind where you don't just stop drinking; you change what drinking was doing for you. This is the phase of honest self-reflection, learning new coping skills, and replacing old reflexes with better ones.

Think of it in three stages:

1. Caterpillar (pre-change): stuck in a pattern, living inside a loop.
2. Chrysalis (change): discomfort, reflection, rewiring, building tools.
3. Butterfly (post-change): improved clarity, resilience, and a healthier relationship with alcohol, often leading to reduced use or sobriety.

Migration

In the context of alcohol, migration refers to intentionally moving from heavy drinking toward moderation or abstinence. Like animals migrating to survive changing conditions, you shift your environment and routines to support your goal.

Migration recognizes that change is dynamic. It can include exploration, setbacks, and progress. The win is direction: you're moving away from what harms you and toward what helps you.

Finding a New Shell

The metaphor of crabs finding new shells reflects the need to replace alcohol with healthier habits. As you grow, the old shell doesn't fit. You don't just drop alcohol, you build a new structure around your life that can actually hold you.

"Finding new shells" can mean new hobbies, new social settings, new coping strategies, and new, stronger relationships. All ways to get stress relief, connection, and pleasure without relying on booze.

Choose one pathway—hibernation, chrysalis, migration, or a new shell—and use it as your blueprint. Don't just wish for change. Pick a model, live it, and let your actions prove it's real.

Advanced Spirit-Animal Transformation Pattern Alternatives

There are more advanced dormancy patterns you can use to quiet the urge to drink and conserve energy. Reaching the next level looks different for everyone. If one or two of these patterns resonate, mark them and journal what they surface. This is about strategy, not poetry.

Estivation: The Strategic Pause

Like hibernation, some animals enter dormancy to survive stress. Estivation is a deliberate shutdown in response to harsh conditions such as heat, drought, or pressure.

Applied to alcohol, estivation means a voluntary pause or sharp reduction in use. Not court-ordered. Not forced. Chosen.

The Art of Sober prefers you enter estivation on your own terms. A DUI and thirty days in the hole locked up will teach you the lesson anyway—but that's the sloppy version. Voluntary restraint is cleaner and cheaper.

Voluntary Pause

You choose to stop or sharply reduce drinking to reassess your habits and regain leverage. Use the time to focus on health, relationships, and forward motion. Journal honestly. No bullshit entries.

Involuntary Pause

Sometimes estivation is imposed upon you. Legal trouble, health scares, money drying up. These pauses arrive fast and hit hard. Learn from others' scars so you don't earn your own. The highway is littered with stories about how someone's life 180°'d and they paused drinking.

Reflection Window

Estivation creates silence. In that quiet, you finally hear the truth about what alcohol costs you. Slow down. Think. Decide.

Recovery and Relapse Defense

Breaking the cycle builds clarity and resilience. Relapse is a grinding tax on time, money, and dignity. This pause helps you build tools before temptation circles back.

Gateway to Treatment

For some, estivation is the entry point to counseling or structured support. Think you can't afford help? Look harder. Pro bono exists. What doesn't exist is progress without effort.

Estivation is not the finish line. It's the regroup.

Daily Torpor: Micro-Wins Matter

Some animals enter daily torpor, a brief energy shutdowns to survive scarcity. In sobriety, daily torpor means short windows of restraint.

That thought at lunch—*'I should grab a beer''*—that's the moment. Let it pass. Don't negotiate.

Where Daily Torpor Shows Up

- Routine: Work hours, family time, structured events. Stay present. Drink water. Don't announce anything.
- Environment: Settings where alcohol isn't central. Keep a non-alcoholic drink in hand and move on.
- Money: Alcohol drains cash fast. Run the numbers. Then run them through a 20-year investment calculator. Sobering, isn't it.

Low-cost hobbies act as guardrails. Woodworking, quilting, running, fixing things, these skills build value instead of hangovers. Communities form. Momentum follows.

Daily torpor alone won't save you, but stacking these small wins builds discipline. That's how patterns break.

Brumation: Controlled Reduction

Reptiles brumate in cold months. It's a slow metabolism with minimal movement. Applied here, brumation means intentional reduction.

Drink less. Not forever—yet—but deliberately. One day matters. Repeat it.

This phase allows tolerance to reset and judgment to sharpen. Say "not tonight" and let your mind either settle or focus hard. That first win becomes the benchmark you beat next time.

Aestivation: Becoming Just You

Aestivation is deep dormancy during extreme conditions. Metaphorically, it's abstinence without identity theatrics.

At some point, you stop saying *"I'm sober"* and simply live that way. You don't announce everything you don't do. Drinking becomes background noise—irrelevant.

If someone offers a beer, respond calmly:

"Got a soda?"

That's it. No speech. No sermon. Control stays with you. Sobriety doesn't need branding. It needs consistency and authority.

Final Note

These patterns, estivation, torpor, brumation, are tools. Not labels. Not lifestyles. Choose one. Test it. Adjust. Animals survive by conserving energy during stress. You can do the same. Pause. Regroup. Move forward with intent.

Quiet strength beats chaos every time.

Next: Choose Your Creature

Now that we've covered hibernation and its variations, it's time to choose your creature. It doesn't have to be perfect. It just has to resonate. Identification accelerates progress. When your mind has something concrete to latch onto, behavior follows more easily.

Animals live by instinct. Their survival depends on automatic responses. Ask yourself this: do you automatically reach for alcohol? You didn't at six years old. It was introduced later, absorbed into your environment, and slowly became part of your ecosystem. Now you're living inside it.

These frameworks aren't cute metaphors. They're tools. Ways to rewire behavior by borrowing instincts that already work in nature. Reduction and abstinence are both valid paths here. Pick what fits your goal and move.

Adopt the Sloth's Pace

Slow everything down. As you work towards your sobriety, if you drink, sip deliberately. Pause between drinks. Check in with yourself before the next one. Most overdrinking happens on autopilot. Sloths don't rush and neither should you.

Mimic the Camel's Conservation

Camels ration resources. You should too. Set hard limits on quantity and timing. Decide in advance. Stick to it. Discipline beats willpower every time.

Channel the Bear's Hibernation

Bears withdraw when conditions are harsh. Design alcohol-free days, weeks, or seasons. Use that time for rest, health, and focus.

And a quick reality check: don't be the sloppy caricature, wine-at-soccer "Mama Bear" or the beer-guzzling Joe Six-Pack starter kit. Both are lazy identities. Just be the bear. Strong. Grounded. Respected by your kids and yourself. Leave the overpriced copy cat thermos of the season filled with booze at home. We all know that a grape Gatorade bottle at a 7p soccer game has wine in it.

Model the Hummingbird's Precision

Hummingbirds refuel without excess. If you're moderating, alternate alcohol with non-alcoholic drinks. Set a minimum of 15–20 minutes per drink. Or better yet, skip it entirely. You don't need a pregnancy or be at rock bottom to stop, just a decision.

Embrace the Butterfly's Transformation

This isn't a flip of a switch. It's a slow process. Set realistic goals. Track progress. Celebrate small wins. Transformation compounds over time into amazing results.

Embody the Dolphin's Social Intelligence

Dolphins survive through connection. Build relationships that support your reduction or sobriety. Anyone who mocks your effort gets distance—fast.

Guard the Three Lives

Everyone has a public life, a private life, and a secret life. The secret one is where habits rot. Sneaking drinks isn't fooling anyone, especially you. What starts hidden eventually spills into everything else.

False connection is a trap. Oversharing at bars. Trauma-dumping on strangers. Posting personal business online. None of it builds real bonds. Keep your discipline quiet. Let results speak. Get offline as much as possible.

Follow the Wolf Pack Code

Wolves thrive through loyalty and structure. Choose a pack that respects your boundaries and reinforces your standards.

Supportive is the keyword. Funny enough, some of the toughest groups, biker clubs, crews, teams all enforce sobriety, usually better than families because rules matter. Think like that. Hold yourself to standards. Reward discipline. You don't need to announce it. Quiet power travels farther.

Take the Cat's Curiosity

Cats explore without commitment. Be curious. Try new hobbies, environments, and routines without alcohol. Curiosity turns mistakes into lessons, stagnation into choice, and progress into momentum.

Bottom Line

Recovery isn't binary. You start, stop, stumble, adjust. Anyone who tells you otherwise is selling something. Eventually, you stop "recovering" and just live. You'll know when you're there.

Nature doesn't rush evolution. Neither should you. Choose a creature. Apply the instinct. Move forward deliberately.

Alternatives: The Elements

If animals aren't your thing, use the elements. Same concept. Different languages.

Earth — Stability

Ground yourself. Walk outside. Touch real things. Build a calm home environment. Use routines and mindfulness to stay centered. Start yoga. Get crazier and do hot yoga.

Water — Flow

Adapt without numbing. Swim. Bathe. Journal. Let emotions move instead of bottling them. "Go with the flow" wasn't a joke, it was survival wisdom.

Air — Clarity

Breathe. Walk. Reflect. Communicate honestly. Distance gives perspective. Perspective kills impulse. Put yourself into calming situations as best as possible.

Fire — Transformation

Set intentions. Pursue goals. Train your body. Create heat in your life that isn't alcohol-fueled. Fire transforms or destroys. Choose wisely. Don't scorch earth everything.

You can mix these systems. Bear plus Earth. Dolphin plus Water. Predator plus Fire. Build a framework that fits you. This isn't about identity theater. It's about leverage. Choose your creature—or your element—and act accordingly.

Advanced Layering of the Elements: Lowering the Load

Let's go a level deeper. Highlight what resonates and discard the rest. This is not doctrine, it's leverage. This is just a suggestion.

Across belief systems, the four elements—air, earth, fire, and water—represent fundamental forces of both nature and human physiology. When applied correctly, they help reduce **allostatic load**: the cumulative wear and tear on your nervous system caused by chronic stress, poor recovery, and repeated alcohol use. Less load means clearer thinking, steadier mood, better sleep, and fewer reactive decisions. By aligning with nature's regulatory systems of elements, cycles, connection, and restraint, you reduce allostatic load and reclaim control. That's the real prize.

Mindfulness (Air)

Mindfulness brings oxygen back to your decision-making. It increases awareness, slows reactivity, and lowers impulsive stress responses. Practically, it means noticing the moment *before* you drink.

Ask simple questions:

- Will this interfere with reading my kid a book in 30 minutes?
- Will this drag into the rest of my day?
- Is this adding stress later to relieve stress now?

Alcohol spikes short-term relief while increasing long-term load. Mindfulness interrupts that loop. This is not spiritual fluff, it's nervous-system management.

Balance (Earth)

Balance stabilizes the system. When physical, emotional, and mental inputs are aligned, alcohol loses its grip. Skip the brunch mimosas if the rest of your day matters. One buzz early destabilizes the entire rhythm. Balance isn't deprivation, it's sequencing. Protect the downstream hours.

Transformation (Fire)

Fire destroys and forges. You can quit outright or burn selectively, either works if it's intentional.

But here's the rule: **removal without replacement fails**. If you stop drinking, replace it with movement, learning, training, service, something that builds capacity instead of draining it. Alcohol increases allostatic load. Purpose lowers it.

Nourishment (Water)

Water restores. Nourishment isn't just food, it's relationships, meaning, contributions. Call your mother. Ask her questions that matter. Nourish and cleave your spouse, your kids, your community. If alcohol has hollowed those relationships out, you already know. Fixing them reduces emotional stress far more effectively than a drink ever did. And if some people reject you when you improve? Good. That's stress leaving your system. Let them go.

By aligning with nature's regulatory systems of elements, cycles, connection, and restraint, you reduce allostatic load and reclaim control. Let's look at more components to enhance your control in recovery.

Connection

Isolation raises allostatic load. Connection buffers it. Build relationships that reinforce your decision, not ones that test it. Community replaces the false regulation alcohol provided. You don't need everyone, just the right few.

Resilience

Resilience is stress tolerance without collapse. It's built by refusing the easy out repeatedly. Alcohol wants you because it's a shortcut. You don't need it. Declining it consistently is how resilience compounds. This becomes your edge. Your serrated edge, your investment in yourself compounding.

Self-Reflection

Reflection lowers background noise. Review your days. What added energy? What drained it? What didn't matter at all? Journal where you feel it is needed. Review as well.

You don't need guilt, just data. Patterns reveal themselves when you look.

Intention

Clear goals reduce cognitive load. Vague goals increase it. You don't have to quit forever today. Reduce frequency. Reduce volume. Measure the effect. Let your nervous system feel the difference. Work towards your goals.

Aligning With Nature, Not Fighting Yourself

Nature regulates stress efficiently. You should too.

Seasons

Match behavior to cycles. More movement, light, and social activity and less alcohol. Your body already knows how to do this once the poison is removed.

Nourish the Body

Eat real food. Drink water. Alcohol blocks nutrient signaling and recovery. Once removed, cravings recalibrate. You won't crave "fun"—you'll crave fuel. We could write an entire chapter on how to eat better. Do your own research, but eat better.

Yin and Yang

This is not binary. Progress includes friction, mistakes, recalibration. That's normal physiology, not failure. Allostatic load drops when perfectionism dies.

Natural Beauty

Get outside. Nature lowers cortisol. This isn't poetic, it's measurable. If you won't change your environment, it will keep changing you. But it's cold outside. Stop being a pussy and connect with natural beauty. Storms reshape landscapes, horizons, rivers and lakes. So can you. Slowly or violently, your choice.

Renewal

Forests are managed. Dead wood is cleared to allow growth. Manage your internal forest. Cut what no longer serves. Plant what will serve short term and long term. Be the person that plants their proverbial tree that will provide shade to their families long after they are dead. Be purposeful.

Limits

Your body keeps score. Mood swings, fatigue, anxiety, these are signals. Alcohol overrides them temporarily, then amplifies them later. Respect the limits. Get off the rollercoaster.

Gratitude

Gratitude lowers baseline stress. That's neuroscience, not sentimentality. Slow down. Appreciate the ordinary. Stop chasing cheap dopamine. Make this a cornerstone and things will amplify for the better. Having gratitude is good. Being grateful is a state.

Interconnectedness

Your drinking affects more than you. So does your discipline. Everything ripples. Choose the ripple you want to create. Just ask a person close to you about a memory of you from a recent outing that included drinking. What you uncover may surprise you.

Summary

By aligning with nature's regulatory systems of the elements, cycles, connection, and restraint, you reduce allostatic load and reclaim control. This is not about identity or purity. It's about **lowering stress, increasing capacity, and living with intention**.

Choose what fits. Discard what doesn't. Move forward in your recovery deliberately. Up and to the right!

That's your new sober blueprint.

4. Weak Points and Strong Points in Your Blueprint

Opportunities arise from the gaps in the environment. These gaps are due to the weakened authority of alcohol. How you react to changes in your journey to sobriety matters. Here we will delve into a great mind and his assessments as it relates to your alcohol abstinence. In your recovery journey, we want you to stay strong, and be aware of the weak points.

Jung, Individuation, and the Call Away from Alcohol

Carl Gustav Jung (1875–1961) was a Swiss psychiatrist, psychotherapist, and founder of analytical psychology. A prolific writer and deep thinker, Jung is best known for his work on archetypes, individuation, and the unconscious. Alongside Freud and Adler, he shaped modern psychology, influencing not only academic thought but spiritual and cultural inquiry as well.

Many of Jung's ideas apply directly to the decision to step away from alcohol, not as a moral failing to be corrected, but as a signal of psychological maturation. What follows is a paraphrased exploration of Jungian themes as they relate to your strengths, struggles, and emerging new relationship with alcohol. Other teachers may also resonate with you, but Jung offers a powerful lens for understanding why this change is arising now.

The impulse to stop drinking is not random. In Jungian terms, it reflects unconscious material surfacing before the conscious mind fully understands it. You may feel disoriented, as if the logic that once guided you no longer holds. Life may seem to be unraveling. What if this confusion is not collapse, but preparation. A necessary dismantling before a truer self can emerge? The danger is not the dismantling itself, but mistaking it for failure, relapse, or bad timing, and numbing the tension with alcohol just before insight breaks through.

You are here reading about sobriety because your inner world is awake. Even if clarity has not fully arrived, the signs are present. You are standing at a threshold.

Jung described several signs that life is not falling apart but reorganizing around a deeper order. If even a few are present, individuation—the unfolding of the authentic self—has begun.

The first sign is questioning what you once accepted as truth. The belief that you could not live without alcohol begins to loosen. This questioning is not disorientation; it is initiation. Like a seed cracking underground, growth begins long before it is visible. Your former life may feel hollow. That discomfort is not something to escape, it is early clarity taking shape. Stepping away from alcohol is not punishment; it is purification. You are not broken. Your strength lies in listening beneath the noise as your authentic self begins to awaken.

The next sign is a sense of disconnection from who you used to be. This can feel unsettling, and resistance here often fuels relapse. Begin again without self-judgment. Identity shedding is subtle. What once excited you may now feel empty. This is not resentment toward sobriety but inevitability. Alcohol's grip is loosening. This is a sign of readiness to grow.

This detachment is not cynicism; it is individuation, a release from inherited beliefs, cultural scripts, and ego defenses. Uncertainty masks clarity. Old personas fall away, and grief may follow. You may ask who you are without them. There will be mourning, possible doubt about the masks you wore in your past life. Questions of weakness will arise such as who are you without your past masks and what matters now. Those questions make space for what is emerging.

You are not broken, you are now becoming. This is not the weakness of failure, but the strength that precedes your transformation into sobriety. You are not failing; you are becoming. Trust this disconnection.

A third sign appears when what once seemed essential—status, approval, achievement, even alcohol—loses its authority. You begin to measure life not by accumulation, but by nourishment and inner resonance. Worth detaches from performance and material things. This recalibration lowers internal strain, easing the chronic stress load carried by the nervous system. New people and opportunities align with this shift. Nothing false will feel like home again.

Another sign is a renewed connection to intuition. Alcohol once dulled it; sobriety strengthens it. Decisions feel less like dilemmas and more like alignments. Mental noise decreases as you stop negotiating life under alcohol's influence. The psyche settles. This internal quiet is not emptiness; it is regulation. Your inner compass realigns, offering calm confidence even when the future remains unclear. There will be less noise in your mind as you are no longer negotiating life under the influence and authority of alcohol. The theater of the mind begins to change to clarity. Even when your future is unclear, you possess a quiet confidence guiding your steps. There is wisdom within you deep and it reveals you to yourself.

A quiet fire sign. Growth becomes necessary, not fashionable. You seek expansion, not entertainment and distractions. This isn't for knowing, but to remember who you are, beneath the layers of conditioning over the years. This is the time when your embodiment awakens and says I cannot remain asleep in the alcoholic state any longer. You may explore forgotten passions, suppressed potentials, and the hidden regions of your life pulling forward towards healing. Wounds once numbed by alcohol are re-understood as initiations. This is individuation: integrating light and shadow into a coherent whole. Sobriety becomes devotion, not deprivation.

Questioning is a sign. You will begin to ask questions that do not come from the ego, such as how do I become successful or how do I appear to others, but rather, what am I to become, what part of me is still waiting to be lived going forward. These questions should not shame you, they are being asked to further awaken you. This is not destruction; it is integration. You will stand apart from the crowd as it means standing closer to your authentic self. The theater of the mind and its masks slip away, and in its place something beautiful emerges - your truth. This is not the peak, this is the threshold, crossing into a life not led by fear, but by purpose. You are ready to grow, heal, become. You will continue to grow into it from within. The fact that you are getting sober proves the seed has been planted.

Detachment signs become prevalant. With this shift comes the urge to leave toxic relationships and familiar patterns that once felt normal. You realize some people were not your companions, they were mirrors of your stagnation. You begin to see how you once tolerated disrespect cloaked as love, confusion disguised as loyalty, and emotional instability accepted as normalcy. These old patterns will feel foreign to the newly sober you, not because they have changed, but because you have. You are no longer a match for them because you have shifted your frequency from them, resonating something purer, quieter, aligned with who you are becoming as a sober entity. This does not come from resentment, but from your revelation of your authentic self, your peace is non-negotiable and you are not a dumping ground. You no longer need to shrink, explain yourself, or fit in to achieve a false harmony, you are choosing yourself out of reverence to the truth you are uncovering from within. This is the shedding of the false self of you written by others, returning to yourself. As you continue to create a distance over time, you see with sharper eyes, you feel with cleaner senses, you begin to crave authenticity over familiarity, you want presence over pretense. Letting go hurts.

You are not losing people, you are losing illusions. You are not breaking bonds, you are breaking cycles. This process is not rejection, it is a redirect. As your landscape becomes more honest, your life begins to mirror that transformation. The best stage of your life does not begin with arrival, it begins with release. The release of alcohol and the grip it has on you.

Interestingly enough, nothing on the outside may look different to the casual observer, but within, the inner landscape is shifting. In this subtle uncoupling lies a deeper truth: this is not avoidance; it is reclamation. You are not running away from anything, you are returning to yourself. In that return, you begin to recognize that freedom is not the absence of responsibility, but the presence of alignment with the Self. You long to be whole. Anything that fractures this clarity falls away. Surrender to what is leaving so that what is emerging may take its rightful place.

This is the mystery of the threshold between sober and not sober, the liminal space Jung described as the crossing between identities, between lives. It is not a loss; it is a passage, clearing the soil for a new psychic order to take root. This shift is real. The old self, shaped by habit, avoidance, and false adaptation, is dissolving. What emerges is truer, more integrated, and resonant. This is the quiet beginning of what you were born to become. Sobriety marks a profound reordering of your inner world, widening the aperture of consciousness and restoring balance where alcohol once distorted perception. Clarity is no longer bound by the authority of the substance, but guided by awareness. This is initiation—not into deprivation, but into a deeper state of being. The signs have been present since you began living alcohol-free. This is an invitation to engage life with eyes and heart fully open. You no longer seek merely to survive, but to live with intention, grace, and authenticity. This is the moment when the architecture of the old persona loosens and the blueprint of something more essential begins to take shape.

Transformation does not come from pretending to be better, but from integrating what is real. The path ahead does not demand perfection; it demands presence. It does not require fearlessness; it calls for honesty with oneself. The most vital stage of your life is not found outside you, but forged through inward turning, where wisdom arises not from answers, but from awareness, and from releasing what no longer serves the psyche's growth. This unfolding is not about becoming more, but becoming more whole. You are not alone on this journey. Together, we move forward in the work of sobriety as individuation. This is not a continuation of the past, but a return home to the authentic Self. The truth has been patiently waiting within you all along.

Strategy, Individuation, and the Long Game of Sobriety

You will fight to be sober on your own terms.

Know alcohol's principles and tactics, but do not advertise your strategy. Alcohol is everywhere; it saturates social life. Recognizing that constant exposure exists is not defeat, it is awareness. You are on a battlefield, awake to the institution of alcohol, and you are crafting a strategy that becomes the foundation of your life going forward.

You will build tools to fortify that strategy. Breakthroughs may be rare at first. Progress often looks like attrition—small wins across many encounters.

I am winning the battle, and I was _______________.

Fill in the truth.

Your strategy is allowed—required—to evolve, because the enemy never approaches in a fixed form. Today it's happy hour; tomorrow it is a birthday; next year a vacation on the beach with drinking involved. Adaptation is mastery. Command your tactics, and you captain your own destiny.

There is no single remedy. People differ in background, beliefs, and resources, yet the aim is the same: sobriety. The battle is mental as much as physical. Debating which matters more misses the point, you need both. Willpower belongs in your arsenal, but alcohol is clever. It exploits fatigue, habit, and stress.

Avoid what is strong; strike where you are strong.
Know your vulnerabilities and your assets. Stack strengths into shields. Volunteering as the designated driver adds structure and removes negotiation. Doing familiar activities sober rewires expectation. You do not *need* wine with dinner because a magazine said so. Skipping weekday beers supports weight, sleep, and mood. Compound outcomes by removing alcohol from the equation.

Question every suggestion of alcohol. The answer is simple: it does not improve the situation. Alcohol's tactic is authority, whispering to you that life is better with it. It isn't. Each refusal reduces internal friction, lowers physiological stress, and lightens the allostatic load your system has been carrying.

Do not let alcohol impose on your existence, your well-being, fortitude, or constitution.

Secure positions that cannot be attacked
Practically, this means changing the pattern: new activities without booze, kept consistent until they are normal. As each alcohol-free routine holds, influence wanes. Handling varied scenarios without alcohol becomes the default. This is individuation in action: fewer masks, less inner conflict, steadier regulation. The war quiets as the strategy holds.

5. Engage the Substance and Win
The Power of Two Degrees and Your Being

Two degrees is a deceptively powerful concept. We're repackaging it as a way to engage alcohol, not with brute force, but with leverage.

At two degrees, things move. A ball barely rolls, yet momentum begins. Change the body's temperature by two degrees and you're sick. Raise the heat in a crowded car by two degrees and irritation spikes. On paper, two degrees looks trivial. In practice, it compounds outcomes.

That's the point.

What happens when friends speak to you two degrees less over time? One month feels negligible. Six months later, connection thins. Two degrees is not dramatic, but it is directional. This approach favors managed momentum over shock.

At some point, you shifted from not drinking to drinking. Maybe slowly. Maybe hard. However you arrived here doesn't matter. What matters is where you're going. The goal isn't to become "sober" as a label. The goal is to *be*. Labels create friction. Being creates equilibrium.

Homeostasis—your sober baseline existence—is not pretend. It's real. Relapse, if it happens, is an event, not your identity. Jung would call this individuation: separating the self from borrowed roles and false definitions. Stop narrating yourself. Just live with conviction. Small two-degree wins matter. Stack them. Compare yourself only to yourself. Someone will always be better-looking, richer, smarter, taller, skinnier. What a bunch of assholes! Fret not. That comparison is noise. Reduce it. Lowering that internal chatter lowers your allostatic load, the wear and tear of constant self-judgment.

If something bothers you, fix what's fixable. Dress better. Cut your hair. Manage expectations. Stop rehearsing the same internal self directed insults. They drain energy you need elsewhere. WHY do you think you are ugly? Unpack that and get to some bottom line reasons why you THINK you are ugly. Five Why's in action. You wear sloppy clothes? Ok, stop doing that. You don't wash your hair often because it is hard to manage and too long? Get it cut to manage it. Sick and tired of your nails not looking good? Maybe start managing the expectations. Stop having that internal negative conversation. It is degrading you. Think you need a new backpack to take stuff to work? Hold up - you are 42 years old. You're a grown adult. Backpacks are for kids, man. Get mature.

Life is interconnected. When you're present—really present—you notice it. Light, sound, movement, sensation, breath. You're not separate from the system; you're in it. Two degrees shifts everything. Angle, temperature, timing. Ships miss ports. Planes miss runways. Small deviations matter.

You will discover how simple and profound the interconnectedness of your life truly is. Standing on a beach at sunset, the ocean meets the sky, clouds drifting or dissolving without announcement. Birds pass in and out of view. A few older men shuffle by in white New Balance shoes. You *see* everything.

Waves break. Conversations murmur in the distance. Sound overlaps sound. The air carries salt, sand, and something indefinable but familiar. If you're barefoot, grit and water press against your feet, cool and insistent. None of it exists in isolation. Each sensation informs the next.

The experience is whole. Everything is connected.

\You are, quite literally, two degrees of separation from the Sun and the Moon. Your feet are in the water. You exist within the atmosphere. The Sun and Moon move through that same system. You are connected.

Two degrees of an angle and the sun slips from view. Two degrees of temperature and water begins to freeze or melt. The change may be gradual, but it is possible. Two degrees may seem insignificant on paper, yet its effects are undeniable.

Living at two degrees is often enough. It doesn't require drastic reinvention—no need to shave your head or dye your hair platinum unless that's your move. In far more serious terms, two degrees of a gun's aim can determine life or death. Two degrees off course on a ship's navigation over hundreds of miles can land you in an entirely different country. Small moves matter.

This is how you should approach drinking: through two-degree adjustments. Small, deliberate shifts. Incremental changes that compound over time. Find *your* two degrees, the one adjustment that nudges you toward limiting, reducing, or stopping altogether. Then build from there.

Change your habits in manageable increments. That's how momentum begins.

Your greatest challenge isn't the routine—work, kids, chores—it's the downtime. The "reward." The pour. It's mind-boggling, but yet, even just the mere act of pouring the wine is the start of satisfaction for many. They may or may not take on a different persona, but that first act is the trigger. They poured the glass. Anticipation alone triggers stress responses: impatience, irritability, shallow focus. The ritual itself becomes the hit you are wanting. Ask the hard question: *Do I actually deserve this drink, or am I just soothing friction I haven't addressed?*

Over time, familiarity breeds contempt and becomes automation. You function on robotic autopilot, mistaking habit for control. Until something external defines the moment such as health, family, the judge sentencing you on your 2nd DUI? Why wait for that?

You don't need catastrophe to change. You need awareness and direction. Two degrees at a time.

Some people taper. Some stop cold. Either method can work for people. The process to sober is personal.

Measure what matters to *you*: sleep, clarity, mood, relationships, weight, pride. Pick one to three metrics. Improve them. Build a strong 90 day plan, achieve what you can. Journal. Then raise the bar. Smaller increments of achievements.

There will be flat tires. Breakups. Dog shitting on the new carpet at the worst possible moment during the football game. Kids vomiting on you. Snow to shovel, wrong food brought to the table. Life happens. You'll handle it without reaching for the old reflex.

Two degrees. Adjust. Hold the line. Momentum will follow.

Engage the Substance

You must sit down with your vice. Not theatrically. Not dramatically. Strategically.

Think of it as a private confession—not to your parents, who may mean well but cannot fight this battle for you; not to your friends, who are busy avoiding their own reckoning; and not even to your spouse at first. Too much early dependence creates weakness. This engagement begins with you. Alone. Clear-eyed.

Engaging the substance doesn't mean dumping every bottle down the drain or writing moral notes on your beer cans. It means studying alcohol as it exists in your life. Its patterns, tactics, timing, and pressure points. Sun Tzu was famously explicit: *"If you know the enemy and know yourself, you need not fear the result of a hundred battles."*

Alcohol is not neutral. It is organized, funded, protected, and omnipresent. Treat it accordingly.

Each person's engagement will look different, but the principle is the same: **turn avoidance into intelligence**. Make quitting, or reducing, an active discipline. Flip the script. Let *not drinking* become the hobby, the experiment, the practice. Keep your enemy close enough to observe without letting it command you.

Many believe alcohol does not interfere with their lives. That belief often rests on low self-awareness, a fortified ego, and habit disguised as control. Alcohol excels at lowering awareness while increasing confidence, the perfect recipe for internal erosion. Chronic exposure keeps your nervous system on constant alert, quietly increasing allostatic load: elevated stress hormones, poor sleep, shortened patience, and diminished recovery. You may feel functional, but your system is paying interest.

This is why education matters. Not fear-based sermons. Intelligence.

Know the enemy:

- Alcohol has unlimited marketing resources.
- It is shielded by lobbyists across governments worldwide.
- Millions unconsciously recruit on its behalf—through jokes, rituals, celebrations, and casual pressure.
- It is highly present in entertainment outlets

In a single day, you may encounter alcohol hundreds of times through media alone. If you tracked it honestly, from billboards to radio, tv shows to movies, gas stations to music lyrics, you would see the pattern clearly. Alcohol is positioned as reward, relief, identity, belonging. This is not accidental.

The One-Day Enemy Pattern Study

Notice what you see, hear, and absorb from wake-up to bedtime. Billboards on the commute. Radio chatter about hangovers. Music lyrics that casually glorify numbness. Social media posts that have 5 dorks all holding up a beer celebrating just being. Store layouts that place alcohol front and center while healthy eating essentials are sidelined. This is psychological terrain. And you are walking through it daily.

The Art of Sober does not advise charging blindly into enemy territory. We advise mapping it first. These outlets do not want to move any martini. They prefer to keep it front and center.

Engaging the substance means reducing surprise. Fewer ambushes. Fewer stress spikes. Lower allostatic load. When the nervous system is no longer constantly negotiating temptation, it begins to stabilize. Clarity increases. Reaction time slows. Choice returns.

This is not moral warfare. It is a strategic withdrawal from a system designed to exhaust you.

Know the terrain. Know the enemy. Preserve your energy.

That is how you win. Spend a day just noticing how pervasive alcohol is in a normal 24 hour period. It'll go something like so.

Billboards and radio hit you on the way to work. Gas station LED signs flash while you fill up. You go inside for coffee—notice where the booze lives. Front and center. Party-in-a-bucket cans stacked at eye level while milk and water hide in the back like bad relatives. Count the glass doors: booze versus Coke, Pepsi, milk. It isn't subtle. Six to eight glass doors from top to bottom with all the alcohol choices you can handle.

Back in the car. Thirty-minute commute. DJs joking about hangovers and drunk party stories. Flip to music—holy shit. Rap, country, rock, pop—nearly all of it nods to booze. Some songs are so creatively bankrupt they talk about beer the entire time. You listen anyway. Mindlessly. That's not coincidence; that's media message creep. It lowers resistance, spikes stress, and quietly adds to your allostatic load before you've even clocked in.

They think you're stupid. Time to engage the substance and prove you're not.

A 2018 analysis of 2,840 top-performing songs found alcohol mentioned in **40% of country music**, compared to **14% in pop, 10% in dance/electronic**, and **9% in rock**. That's not culture, that's commerce. Follow the money long enough and you'll see how entertainment, alcohol, and financial stakeholders are stitched together. If you know what the VIX is, you already understand volatility systems. If you don't, this is your wake-up call. The system wants you to be volatile. Volatility leads to profit.

Once you realize the system profits from keeping you dulled, distracted, and stressed, you stop cooperating. Like someone finally recognizing abuse for what it is. Clarity and context changes everything. We move on.

You arrive at work. Office, warehouse, shop floor—it doesn't matter. Monday or Friday, the chatter circles around booze. Weekend drinks. Last night's beer bash by the fire. A couple of jackasses trying to intellectually debate whiskey brands like anyone gives a shit. They're stealing your time and jacking your nervous system for free. Scan the environment: office fridge, desk drawers, parking lot. Look for Gatorade bottles that aren't Gatorade. "Grape flavor" is their wine in the bottle, trust us. Brown paper bags. People hide addictions until laziness gives way and they really just don't care anymore. Their car will be crammed with all sorts of bottles or styro cups that once kept their secret life secret.

Lunch break. Radio on. More booze threaded into songs. Restaurant choice? Neon beer signs everywhere. Coasters, napkins, menus, wall art—alcohol is branded into the furniture. Bars are designed so you *see everything alcoholic.* Shirts, lame ass slogans, décor—it's a full on sensory assault. More background stress. More allostatic load.

Back to work. Now you can't unsee it. By afternoon, booze imagery auto-highlights in your brain. Newspapers. Magazines. Influencers on screens. It's relentless.

Drive home—say it's Friday. You pass eight dive bars. Parking lots packed. Neon signs promise "fun." Society tells people Friday is freedom and booze is freedom from the gatekeeper. Working for the weekend has been beaten into heads so much that some of these folks are in their own self-induced mental institution. Remember, you cannot fix stupid. Don't try. This is about you and only you. You have to detach. That weekly cycle is poison for anyone trying to quit anything. Living for weekends hard-codes stress spikes and crash cycles into your body. Doers don't live by weekends off. They live by intention.

You don't need heroics. You need strength. Two degrees at a time is fine—but forward only. Start breaking non productive *non-alcohol habits* first. Screen scrolling time. Nightly news for more than 1 hour. Endless sports chatter on ESPN. Replace, reduce, eliminate. Build the muscle of change. Every broken habit frees time, energy, and nervous-system bandwidth. Declutter with purpose.

Back to your drive home. More ads. "Chill," says the Coors billboard. No—you don't need to chill, you need to stop being programmed.

You are now home. You shower. You go out for a burger with a couple of buddies. Order a beer. Chewing gum? Spit it out. Don't be that guy who chews and drinks at the same time. Billiards, burgers, beers, staring at women who aren't interested in you one iota. Conversations with your lads that teach you nothing. Track it mentally: are you getting smarter or dumber as the night goes on? Many simply say they are recharging or blowing off steam to justify it. Weak.

A woman talks to you. Now observe the differences. Are you sober? You're present. Cutting back? You can slow it down. Are you drinking and 4-6 beers deep into the night? You're floating in a booze-fogged dream, mistaking chemistry for booze laden connection. That isn't romance—it's ethanol.

The bar closes. You go home. You wake up hungover.

You already know how this movie ends. Same plot. Different day. Booze as a placeholder. Time slipping away.

Remember this: **you don't have time, time has you**.

Engage the Substance and Treat It For What It Is: Your Enemy

You can reclaim authority from alcohol. It is a massive business. But that is not your concern here. The broader cultural shift away from drinking may be underway, but your work is singular and personal. Change happens one person at a time, and right now that person is you.

Increase your awareness of your own needs as you move through the day. In Jungian terms, this is the ego learning to listen to the deeper self rather than outsourcing authority to habit, culture, or approval. Begin—mentally and physically—to prioritize your needs over external expectations. That may mean temporarily trimming commitments that drain you. For example, skip the playdate. Your three-year-old will not remember missing his friend "Auggie" on a Tuesday, but they will benefit from a regulated, rested, and present parent years from now. This is an investment with real return.

Avoiding alcohol does not need to be about daily combat or martyrdom. Move past the story that casts you as a victim. Alcohol is a product, not a moral referendum. Treat it as such. Just as you would not avoid buying a car you like because of someone else's assumptions, do not avoid sobriety because of imagined judgment. Own the choice. Identity stabilizes when it is claimed, not defended.

At its core, this is about refusing to live inside other people's guardrails. You cannot control their opinions, commentary, or projections. Jung would call this the shedding of borrowed personas, the beginning of individuation. Let others drink what they drink and think what they think. Do not let their noise infiltrate your inner world and add unnecessary strain. Chronic vigilance and self-doubt increase allostatic load; clarity and self-alignment reduce it.

Build and live within your own guardrails. Even people close to you may mock or misunderstand your choices. If the exchange is light and mutual, fine. If it is vindictive or undermining, step away regardless of who they are. Your standards are not negotiable.

Engage the substance on your terms. You do not need to respond to every comment or justify every decision. That way lies exhaustion. Instead, shift your internal frame: alcohol is not a challenge to wrestle with, nor a loss to mourn. It is simply a problem you no longer choose to carry.

That quiet decision made consistently lowers internal stress, restores balance, and creates the conditions for something truer to emerge.

Simply shift your paradigm of thinking that alcohol is a problem.

If it is not present in your daily existence, it does not exist?

Many people unknowingly live by a rule often attributed to Satan: *the greatest trick Satan ever pulled was convincing you he doesn't exist.* They don't realize they're applying it to drinking every day. The greatest trick of alcohol is convincing you it is not the core of your problems, but that other things contribute to your problems, and in fact, alcohol helps you deal with those problems.

Let sobriety work in a similar way. At its cleanest, alcohol simply does not exist in your life—your routines, patterns, growth, or future. It is a physical object out in the ether, nothing more. The real danger is not the bottle; it's the idea of the drink—the emotions, memories, rituals, and false comfort attached to it. That's what drives relapse, or keeps people from quitting at all.

You must block alcohol physically and mentally. Cast it out of your thinking. Repeat. Repeat again. The thoughts will return at first, but over time they lose gravity until they carry no more weight than a fleeting urge to punch some loudmouth in the nose. You notice the thought, then you let it pass. That's regulation. That's lowering allostatic load instead of spiking it.

If you're cutting back or quitting, celebrate progress. Breaking habits takes effort. Pride is earned here.

Nedo Vero - "I see black" is where your shadow is—the blind spot where the false self hides. This is where the real work happens. You let go of the persona that needed alcohol to cope, perform, or belong. Eventually, desire and reality collide, and your sober self comes sharply into focus, no longer in the black of the shadow. This creates a shift in mindset. You'll see your goal clearly: your sober self. The core of this change is the sinthome, which helps you find joy in life by creatively connecting with your experiences. You will no longer trap yourself in alcoholism. You'll break free from the false beliefs that kept you from being sober.

The shift is internal and irreversible. You stop orbiting alcohol and stop negotiating with it.

Your relationship to alcohol changes. You are no longer uncertain or powerless. It simply doesn't exist for you anymore. Whatever mythology once surrounded it—temptation, rebellion, reward—falls apart. When you are sober, you are yourself: authentic, grounded, unfiltered.

Think of it this way: you might fantasize about ramming a terrible driver, but you don't follow them and lose your mind at the next stoplight. Alcohol deserves the same treatment. Make drinking increasingly inconvenient, complex, and unrewarding, until not drinking becomes the default. Progress often accelerates quietly, then suddenly. Don't punish yourself for *thinking* about booze. Moving from dependence to occasional thought is forward motion.

The goal is distance from the center of gravity. Alcohol is a black hole—psychological, emotional, energetic. Step back far enough and its pull weakens. Expand your life instead. New habits, deeper relationships, cleaner routines. Less internal noise. More capacity. That's how stress load drops and equilibrium returns.

You've engaged the substance. Now you starve it. We're giving you tools; you supply the resolve. The fact that you're reading this already matters. One step. Then another. That's how wars are won.

6. Pitfalls and Resistance to Your Goals

Drinking Is a Socially Accepted Handicap

In many cultures, alcohol is celebrated as a social lubricant. Moderate use may be tolerated by some, but treating alcohol as "normal" carries real consequences. Cheap beer at the Union hall or free liquor at the office doesn't mean you have to drink it.

Normalization of Harmful Behavior

When drinking is socially accepted, harmful behaviors get a free pass. Binge drinking. Driving under the influence. Blackouts framed as funny stories. *Everyone does it*, so it must be fine—wrong. Trying to "keep up" with friends proves nothing except your willingness to waste money, memory, and judgment while raising your risk of injury, arrest, or worse. From falling off a barstool to killing yourself, or someone else, alcohol doesn't negotiate. It compounds damage quietly, then all at once.

Peer Pressure and Social Influence

Drinking culture thrives on herd behavior. Bachelorette parties, college events, homecomings, New Year's Eve—the calendar is stacked with alcohol excuses. You're choosing not to cave. That puts you in the 1%. Own it.

Stop tracking what others are doing and look inward. That internal shift lowers stress load and restores agency. Seek out people who drink less, or not at all, and ask real questions. You'll find many want to quit drinking but lack a catalyst. You might become their catalyst. Don't preach. Don't push. Keep it about *you*. If you hear yourself saying "that's crazy" four times, the conversation's over. Walk away.

Alcohol may be the only activity people aggressively pressure others into. Nobody ever bullied you into playing kickball.

Negative Health Consequences

Excessive drinking damages the liver, heart, brain, and increases cancer risk. We all know this, yet normalization dulls urgency. The damage often shows late: bloated bodies, hollow eyes, brittle moods, cognitive fog. Think genetics saved you because you still have abs? Keep telling yourself that. Alcohol always collects interest. Reducing intake lowers chronic stress on the nervous system and helps reset your baseline, your allostatic load drops when the poison does.

Impact on Mental Health

Life is hard enough. Alcohol adds avoidable complexity. Sobriety sharpens thinking, steadies mood, and reduces anxiety loops. In drinking cultures, people avoid addressing alcohol-linked depression or anxiety because it's "just how things are." Meanwhile, the spiral tightens.

You watch a game with friends. You get home and keep drinking. It's 1:15 a.m. on a Tuesday. Work suffers. You get fired. Downward momentum accelerates. This happens every day. Mental health goes first; everything else follows. Your damaged mental health can grip your mind tighter than pantyhose two sizes too small.

Family and Social Relationships

Obvious one here. Drinking strains relationships. Misinterpretations multiply. Trust erodes. Invitations slow, then stop. Sometimes people exclude you because they love you and don't know how to help. At the end of the day (we HATE that expression by the way) they begin to protect themselves and their own relationships, and if that means excluding you as the drinking problem person, they do. Sobriety is the first repair. It won't be instant; people distrust sudden change. Fine. Do sober *you*. Those who matter will circle back. Those who don't, keep moving from them.

Economic Costs

Alcohol drains wallets and societies alike: healthcare, lost productivity, legal costs and property damage. Ask an insurance agent, they'll confirm. When consequences hit your bank account, attention follows. That's why fines are steep. Now they have your attention.

Cultural Influence on Behavior

Turn on music or TV, alcohol is everywhere. It's background noise until it isn't. Subliminal messaging worked in the '70s and it still works now. Trends don't spread because they're smart; they spread because they're repeated. Be above normalization. Disengage from the noise. It's a learned skill, but it's how clarity returns. If you do not think you can be easily influenced, just look at what is trendy 'today' as you read this. It is only trendy because the sheep are adopting the marketing messaging, imagery, and perceived benefits. After a period of time, it becomes normalized.

You can be sober in a sea of salaciousness.

Trying to be like James Bond and drinking martinis can feel cool and sophisticated for a while. Then the newness wears off, and it becomes just another accessory, one you don't even realize you don't need. It may seem like a steak dinner requires a martini before you order and a glass of nice red wine to complement it. That idea was sold to you by the industry. There are other options to pair with a good filet, you just have to find them.

Selling you a dream is the marketer's job. Don't think for one minute it isn't. A billboard that simply states "Liquid Fun" is about as uncreative as it gets, but to a 21-year-old—or really, to anyone—it can seem like that alcohol is now a requirement for having fun. Really. They think you are stupid. You are not stupid, you just see things for what they are now.

Underage Drinking

Social acceptance fuels early drinking. Kids convince themselves they're rebelling, when they're really buying the lie early. Ads did the heavy lifting. The real lesson isn't punishment, it's exposure to the long-term wreckage. Some adults seem "in control." Some are. Many aren't. Don't waste time diagnosing others.

This is about you.

Don't become a sobriety evangelist either. Most people don't care. Most people you know probably don't care about your issues. In fact, 80% won't pay attention. The other 20% might even feel happy that you have problems. Remember, they have their own problems, even if you do not know what they are. Do this for you, no one else. Everyone has problems. Solve yours.

If you're young, build your identity without alcohol. Growth requires focus. Alcohol hijacks energy and attention. Whilst it sounds great to share a glass of whiskey with someone to discuss how they navigated a legal issue or business deal, skip the whiskey and be 100% present in the dialogue. If offered a drink, decline cleanly: *"I want to hear your story—maybe a drink later."*

Moderate drinking may work for some. But treating alcohol as a social norm fuels harm, hides risk, and taxes mental and physical systems. A more honest relationship with alcohol, starting with your own, reduces stress, restores balance, and supports long-term well-being. Move forward. Cut through resistance. Stay sharp.

Revisiting Common Trigger Pitfalls to Drinking (Yes, the Broken Record)

Several common triggers pull people back to alcohol after they've tried to cut back or quit. Triggers are everywhere. Your job isn't to avoid life, it's to anticipate these moments and move through them sober, present, and in control. When you manage triggers, you lower your allostatic load, the cumulative stress that quietly pushes people back to the bottle.

Stress

Stress is the heavyweight champion of relapse. Work, relationships, money, health—people drink to blunt the edge. Fine. Get a stress ball. Read a book. Learn how stress actually works. *The Art of Sober* keeps it simple: if you think you have a problem, go find a bigger one. Stress isn't the enemy, poor stress management is. Breath.

Social Situations

Parties, dinners, outings—booze is treated like an accessory. Until it isn't. Alcohol becomes a crutch fast. You have options: step outside, sit with the kids, change seats, change rooms. Or, here's the wild idea, go anyway and don't drink. A bull runs into the storm. If someone presses you about not drinking, ask calmly, "Are you okay?" That usually shuts it down. If not, excuse yourself. That's a power move.

Emotional Distress

Sadness, anger, boredom, loneliness—these spike cravings. Alcohol promises relief and delivers debt. Create a pause: 90 seconds or three minutes. Step outside. Breathe. Say it out loud if you have to. Emotional regulation is a skill, not a diagnosis. Learn it. It pays dividends long after sobriety. This comes in handy for all types of situations. Don't get so nutty people want to 5150 you. Keep your composure and get through the trigger.

Environmental Cues

Passing old bars. Seeing ads. Remembering "the good old days." We weren't thinking, we were drifting. Ahhh the good old days of drinking at the local alcohol abuse dive bars for $1.95 a Jack and Coke in

Chicago. What were we thinking? We weren't, we were just living. No one told us we were wasting away, but it was better than sitting at home playing video games, or was it? We were living the high life, so we thought. Nostalgia lies. Keep moving forward. Take what you liked—connection, movement, novelty—and rebuild it without alcohol. Don't let memory mislead your future.

Negative Self-Talk

Shame, guilt, low self-worth—these drive relapse hard. If you're suicidal, seek help immediately. Full stop. Otherwise, recognize this: alcohol feeds negative inner dialogue and raises your baseline stress until everything feels heavier than it is. Cutting alcohol lowers that internal pressure. Call someone if you have to.

Celebrations and Milestones

Birthdays, holidays, weddings—alcohol is sold as the celebratory reward. Plan ahead. Skip the event if you need to. No one remembers you missing a party a year later, unless it was your own wedding someone else paid for. Choose wisely.

Peer Pressure

Tell one goblin you quit drinking and the whole underworld knows. Some people will mock you. Fuck them. Others will quietly disappear. Good. You just gained X-ray vision. Real friends stick around. It's fine to decline booze-soaked events, you're not better than them, just on a different vector. Small 2° shifts add up.

Lack of Support

Isolation increases relapse risk. Support systems matter. Tools belong in your shed, use them, swap them, eventually outgrow them. What works now may not work later. That's not failure; it's evolution.

Communicate cleanly and be simpatico. Don't be a dick. If someone gets offended, that's their world, not yours. Maybe find a movie or some media that promotes sober to get the support you need in the moment.

Routine Disruptions

Travel, schedule changes, life shocks—they unsettle recovery. Treat disruption as training, not sabotage. Flexibility lowers stress load and keeps you steady when routines break.

Positive Triggers

Pleasure, relaxation, "just one"—these are sneaky fuckers. Have a comeback ready if someone pushes: "Shots are for kids," or "I took my shot with your mom last night, that was all I needed." That should shut them up, or get your ass kicked. Be prepared, not paranoid. You control you. No celebrity encounter, no moment, no future story is worth derailing your hard-earned progress.

Let's delve a little deeper into less common triggers that go beyond the normal, everyday patterns of life. Esoteric triggers are subtle factors that can lead to alcohol use. They often relate to deeper, subconscious, or spiritual aspects of a person's mind or surroundings. Though not easily seen, recognizing these triggers is key to a full recovery.

Spiritual Disconnection

Emptiness drives escape. Find quiet. Yoga works. Just don't join a cult. Connection reduces inner noise and stabilizes the nervous system.

Past Trauma (Real Trauma)

Unresolved wounds matter. Therapy, groups, holistic work—use what helps. But know your definitions. Not every bad memory is trauma. If you looked at your Mom's magazines under her mattress and thought only dudes got naked and did certain things, because that is all you saw, that is not trauma. That is your parents fault for not educating you and you not paying attention in middle school health education classes.

Public, Private, and Secret Life

Take responsibility for your private life. Public behavior can be corrected; secret behavior compounds.

Don't blame others for your "private and secret" life. That is on you—100%. What you do in public can be judged, corrected, and learned from. What you do in secret, no one sees, so it continues unchecked. Hiding booze in the back of the toilet where the water is stored? Ugh.

Secretly drinking and getting wasted from 8 p.m. to 10 p.m. every night, not answering the phone? The only thing someone may notice is that you're not answering your phone. That's it. Publicly drinking at a bar from 8 p.m. to 10 p.m., however, is visible to everyone there, and you can be sure it will be judged. Falling asleep at the bar is a clear sign of a problem.

If falling asleep at the bar is happening early in your life, it's a good time to hit the reset button and get as far away from alcohol as possible. Trust us. Easier said than done? Yes. But you must.

Existential Anxiety

Meaninglessness fuels drinking. You don't need to "find your place" in the universe, the universe already has you. By exploring life's deeper themes, individuals can find meaning, purpose, and connection. This can help ease anxiety and lessen the urge to self-medicate with alcohol. Engage with it. Purpose lowers anxiety. Anxiety feeds addiction.

Soul Loss, Karma, and the Metaphysical

If these frameworks resonate, explore them. Energy matters. Reflection matters. Write a letter to your future self. Read it later. Progress leaves receipts. You've heard the phrase "do unto others." Start doing unto you. By quitting alcohol, you are doing yourself a favor that your future self will appreciate.

Cosmic Influences

Astrology, meditation, energy work—use what grounds you without numbing you. Alcohol blunts awareness; clarity requires presence.

In Summary: Your Mind and Your Brain.

Pitfalls and resistance to your goals can be understood by distinguishing between the mind and the brain. The mind is intangible; it manifests through perception, reasoning, and memory. The brain, by contrast, is physical, coordinating the body's functions. Your pitfalls and resistance to your goals may or may not be present in your mind. They are truly unique from person to person. They should be treated as such, unlike the brain, which everyone possesses in essentially the same physical form.

At its core, the desire to drink is a mindset in itself, while alcohol is simply a material, physical product that enables alcoholism. Remove the alcohol, and you strip it of its authority over you. What remains is the work of overcoming one or more mental pitfalls, tricks of the mind. That is where the real work lies, and where sobriety is ultimately won.

The mind is energy, and it generates energy through thinking, feeling, and choosing. It is our aliveness, without which, the physical brain and body would be useless. That means we are our mind, and mind-in-action is how we generate energy in the brain. The higher your voltage, the better.

Knowing your mind and brain are separate puts you in the control seat because you can learn to manage your thoughts and actions. Ultimately, it means you can choose what you build into your brain and how you choose to change what's already built in.

When you learn how to manage your mind, you can make feelings of depression, stress, anger, and anxiety work for you instead of against you. You can bring balance back into your brain and life.

Identify your triggers. Build counters. Reduce stress. Stay adaptable. Each trigger handled lowers your allostatic load and strengthens your sober baseline.

This isn't about perfection, it's about staying upright, aware, and moving mindfully forward.

7. Win the Battle. Gather Support Where Needed. Every Day Counts

Start with the low-hanging fruit: your spouse or partner, then parents, siblings, kids, grandkids. But be prepared to stand alone. Everyone has problems, and not everyone can carry yours.

Here's a thought exercise. Imagine you're dropped into the year 1235 or 1690 for a year—period clothes, a little money, nothing else. You land in Ireland or England. You speak the language, but reference things no one understands, such as a cell phone, car, bike, even an airplane. How do you gather support without being labeled a witch or lunatic? You adapt. You observe. You choose allies carefully. That's how support works now.

Choosing sobriety can feel like moving backward in time—explaining yourself, proving intent, convincing others you've changed. Remember: not everyone needs to be 100% sober, and not everyone needs to understand your path.

As you seek support, you will often feel alone. Sometimes help won't be there when you need it. That requires adjustment. Solitude, often mistaken as weakness, is where strength is forged. Jung would call this the turn inward, where authority shifts from the outer world to the self.

Solitude

Solitude is time set aside to think, reflect, and recalibrate. When you're working on difficult goals like reducing or quitting alcohol, it becomes essential. Early on, you may resist it. Later, you'll crave it.

Self-Reflection

Solitude lets you examine your relationship with alcohol: patterns, triggers, motives. Reflect without self-loathing. The past is done. Let it be fertilizer, not a prison. Growth requires purposeful, effective trimming like clearing a forest path, not obsessively pruning a bonsai. You don't need perfection; you need movement.

Clarity of Purpose

When distractions fall away, values sharpen. Purposeful disconnection may mean stepping back from clubs, leagues, gaming marathons, or social obligations for a season. Don't rush to replace them. Clean the slate first. Space matters.

Mindfulness Practice

Solitude is fertile ground for mindfulness and observing thoughts and sensations without judgment. You may ask, "What's the point of this?" That's normal. Over time, your own energy returns, steadier and less desperate. This is why people hunt, fish, bike, or walk alone. Be selfish with this time. The village needs to be fed, but the warrior needs strength.

Emotional Healing and Professional Help

Solitude creates room to process stress, anxiety, trauma, and low self-worth—drivers of drinking. Professional help can be valuable in guiding the process.

Pro tip: book a defined number of sessions. Avoid endless excavation unless that's your aim. Therapy is a business; some practitioners will keep you forever if you let them. Set goals. If it helps, continue. If not, change course.

We at The Art of Sober aren't professional therapists on any level, but we can say this with certainty: some people will take advantage of you. It's a business, after all. Do you have a lot of tattoos, pink hair, piercings on your nose? To the wrong person, you look like a meal ticket from a mile away. Buyer beware. If your IQ is higher than your therapist, get a new one.

There are plenty of great professionals out there. But as the saying goes, *if I cure you, you no longer need what I'm selling.* That should make anyone sick. Some people play that game—that's the way of the world sometimes. Just be aware when they ask YOU if you want to be prescribed any psychotropic medications. That isn't good.

Set a few clear goals and stay focused. If you're finding value, good—keep going. If you're not, walk away and try another path. The right therapist will work on your mind, not your brain. Know the difference.

Personal Growth

Solitude reveals self-imposed barriers. Start small and live at the edge of your comfort zone. Try new foods, walk unfamiliar paths, read outside your lane. Zig when you'd normally zag. As you build muscle memory for breaking barriers, drinking often fades. Failure isn't fatal; it's feedback. If no one dies, you're fine.

Resilience Building

Time alone builds inner strength—the grit needed when temptation hits. It's not easy. Remove phones and pocket devices when possible. Paint, read, build, learn an instrument. Short, focused goals work: learn a song in four weeks, make a gift, build something with your hands, make cookies with a relative. Try telling a story for 90 seconds to someone without using the word "like" out of context.

Creating Boundaries

Solitude helps you set boundaries. If you need a drink to play bingo, trivia, cards, sit around a fire, or be on a float trip you should stop going. Choose activities that set you up to win. You can paint without the wine. Shit, an entire business was built around people painting while drinking wine. I can guarantee those are some of the shittiest paintings you've ever seen. But hey, they got out of the house. By setting boundaries and prioritizing your well-being, you could do the painting without the drinking. Boundaries protect sobriety.

In summary, solitude is a powerful component of your blueprint. It supports self-reflection, mindfulness, emotional healing, growth, resilience, and boundaries. Set small, intentional goals: a short walk, eyes closed in a chair, three extra minutes in a hot shower. Structure the time. Stack with wins. You'll start to want it. This is you, with you. Repeat: *I am, and I was.*

Even Out the Peaks and Valleys
Routine reduces alcohol use by adding structure and accountability. Here are some ways a routine can help in this regard:

Allocate Time for Self-Care
Schedule daily or weekly self-care—exercise, journaling, meditation, or hobbies with a good return on time. The goal is *self*. Lower stress, fewer cravings.

Plan Alternatives
Replace drinking with non-alcoholic plans—coffee, fitness, hobbies. Try to fit some new hobbies in on a Friday or Saturday night without broadcasting it.

Monitor Triggers
Notice when urges hit. Adjust routines. Sometimes avoidance is smart; sometimes you face it prepared. Control beats surprise.

Establish Accountability
Tell one trusted person your plan. Accountability isn't nagging; it's verification. Choose wisely.

Track Progress

Use a journal, app, or calendar. Spot patterns and adjust accordingly. Celebrate wins. Sobriety is a lifestyle, not a fad. If you need to capture a moment to mentally stabilize, do so.

Your surroundings are a reflection of your conscious self, even if you don't realize it yet. Track your progress. As you improve, your awareness grows. You'll notice a reduced need for alcohol and a lower desire for it. This is almost an innate law of being that most people do not realize exists. It becomes a self fulfilling prophecy. Keep on track and sobriety happens.

Practice Consistency

Stick to the routine, especially when you don't want to. Habits compound. When sober muscle memory kicks in, you're on the right path.

Celebrate Achievements

Mark milestones—a week, a month, longer. Celebrate simply, alone or with someone you trust. No speeches required. If getting the coin is what you desire, go for it. If a simple pat on the back is what you crave, get it! Avoid the emptiness of social media for a quick dopamine hit. Journal your milestones, notch your belt, or go out for that ice cream!

Build these elements into your days. Habits take time. Stay patient. Stay committed. The battle is won one day at a time. As you move forward, you will begin to experience higher lows and higher highs, evening out your peaks and valleys up and to the right as time moves forward. *I am and I was* begin to converge into *I am and I am.* Read that again. Understand it.

Domesticate Your Impulses

Domesticating impulses means managing instinctive behavior so it aligns with your values and long-term goals. Sobriety becomes easier when you fulfill your own prophecy of being sober. Fewer impulsive spikes mean less chaos and a lower allostatic load—the cumulative stress your body carries. Turn short sober *moments* (2–5 minutes) into sustained *times* (hours). You're converting jagged urges into steady waves. Here's why domesticating impulses matters:

Self-Control

Impulse control builds discipline. It helps you delay immediate gratification in favor of long-term well-being. Regulating urges leads to intentional choices across life, especially around alcohol, reducing stress on your nervous system.

Improved Decision-Making

When impulses are managed, reason replaces reaction. Consider alcohol: a shot of booze takes seconds and detonates effects fast. Sipping the same amount over an hour blunts the spike. If you do shots, stop. Immediately. Shots are amateur hour. You look like a fucking fool ordering them, doing them, and puking after your third shot while yelling "social" really loud in a shitty bar with a third-rate DJ wearing a K-Mart, sold-by-the-inch gold necklace, playing music on a laptop and just trying to make a buck. It's foolish theater.

Domesticate the urge, and your decisions improve because you're pausing long enough to see consequences play out in real time.

Healthier Lifestyle

Impulse control supports better eating, regular movement, real sleep, and skipping booze. Pairing reduced drinking with basic health choices is a one-two punch for success and a direct way to lower allostatic load.

Diet is simple: calories in versus calories out. Sugar counts. Cookies are fine—eight in ten minutes is not. No need to be a Joey Chestnut at every eating opportunity. Honor your body. Eat well, move more, drink less. Celebrate wins with intention, not excess. Long-term health beats quick rewards.

Enhanced Relationships

Unchecked impulses strain relationships. Pausing builds trust. Try the 10-second rule—not for dropped food, but for conversation. Silence slows the room. Calm spreads. This becomes second nature when sober; alcohol warps timing and tone. We've all seen drunken blowups over nothing. Take me to Milford! Most aren't warranted. Learn when to pause.

Achieving Goals

Impulse control keeps you focused. Domesticating impulses is key to reaching personal and professional goals. It helps people stay focused, motivated, and persistent in their pursuits.

Alcohol is sold as a social lubricant, but it's a professional inhibitor. Work happy hours feel mandatory; they're often catalysts for problems. If you're sober at the happy hour, you see what others miss—good and bad. Stay out of office politics if you are attending. Protect your goals. Don't let booze cost you a job, clients, or credibility.

Financial Stability

Impulse spending breeds debt. Domesticate it. Try a shock tactic: leave cards at home. Carry $50 and your license. Decisions change fast. Ask yourself what that $50 cost you in time and taxes. Drinking burns both time and money. Zoom out.

Reduced Stress and Anxiety

Reactive living fuels anxiety. Managing impulses brings steadiness and resilience, again, lowering allostatic load. People tend to be overwhelmed or underwhelmed. The Art of Sober wants you **whelmed**.

To sum it up, domesticating impulses puts you back in control. It builds self-awareness, discipline, and growth. It may take effort and practice, which can feel uncomfortable at times. The payoff is calm, clarity, and lasting progress.

Learn Your Triggers and Commands

Becoming self-aware of your triggers takes introspection and observation. You must study your patterns. Your thoughts, emotions, and situations that reliably lead to certain behaviors. This is reconnaissance. Know the terrain before you move. Here are some critical steps a person can take to enhance self-awareness of their behavioral triggers:

Mindfulness Practice

Mindfulness—meditation, deep breathing, body scans—brings awareness to what's happening *now*. That awareness lowers reactivity and reduces allostatic load. Find breathing techniques that fit your current state: diaphragmatic, box, lion, or simple deep belly breathing. If you walk 1–2 miles a day, pair it with breathwork. Mindfulness lets you observe thoughts and feelings without judgment, making triggers visible instead of automatic.

Keep a Journal

Journal simply or in detail. Track thoughts, feelings, and daily events. Patterns will emerge especially around drinking.

Think of journaling as backtesting. Investors study past data to see if a strategy worked. Do the same with alcohol. If a Saturday night went sideways *with* drinking, odds are it will again. History repeats for people who refuse to learn from it. If you are above it and do not think history repeats, sure. You will certainly find it rhymes. Some people do not learn from face value. How many times do you need to lose to realize drinking is not a winning strategy. You haven't felt the pain yet, or come to realize a change is maybe needed.

Now, if we told you for every drink you had, we were going to pin prick some random kid in the world, you are now faced with a choice. Many would still drink, figuring the risk - reward is fine. They don't know the kid. Prick that kid! Let's change it up. Every time you drink, we pull a bit of hair from your Mom's head. That lady might go bald in a month if you're not careful. Journal your history and learn from it to reduce or quit your drinking.

Journal how things might have gone *without* alcohol. Pain is a teacher, some people need more of it before they listen. Learn early.

Journaling rules:

- Don't overthink. Write.
- Don't journal only when stressed—capture the good and the bad.
- Reflect to grow, not to narrate the day.
- Re-read with intent, not nostalgia. Schedule it.
- Use entries to build pattern recognition and muscle memory.

Monitor Your Reactions

Watch how you react when emotions spike. Many patterns are deeply ingrained; start small. We're not talking about switching toothpaste brands, just be open to change.

Reaction requires latency. Fear of being taken advantage of, feeling disrespected, these are common triggers. Self-regulation is the skill. The Art of Sober favors an Aikido-style response: redirect the energy back to its source. Echo the trigger back calmly. If someone insults you, repeat their words neutrally. It often disarms the situation. Add breath. Add space. Purposeful latency is productive. Control the response.

Seek Feedback

Ask trusted people for feedback sparingly. A simple check-in like, *"Am I showing up as I should?"* is enough. This creates a feedback loop, useful whether you're cutting back or quitting.

Rules of the feedback oop:

- Choose people you trust.
- Watch for lazy or biased feedback.
- Set a sane frequency—every 4–8 weeks.
- If you slip, don't panic-call everyone. Pause. Breathe. Assess.
- Set guardrails so feedback doesn't turn into a character assassination.

Technology counts too. Wearables give objective data—sleep, heart rate, stress, recovery. That's not philosophy; it's evidence. Use it.

Bottom line: don't rely on one person. Don't become needy. And don't use social media, it's a cesspool, not a compass. Respect your feedback providers; let them opt out when needed. This is a give-and-take. By providing guardrails and tailoring the feedback loop, you are not allowing your provider to take this opportunity to 'and another thing about you I don't think is so great' dump on you. Maybe you mix it up and occasionally let them have fun roasting you. But without guardrails, they may end up roasting you crispier than a duck in Chinatown.

If triggers are giving you serious thoughts of self-harm, call 911 immediately.

Reflect on Past Experiences

Review moments where you reacted impulsively. Ask what really happened and what you *thought* happened. Alcohol distorts perception. Many blowups start with misread cues. Learn the difference. Did you fly off the handle because some guy was licking his lips while facing your general direction and you thought he was making a suggestive pass at you when he was really just trying to clear off his upper lip? We could go on.

Identify Cues

Notice early warning signs—shifts in mood, tension, restlessness. These precede urges. Alcohol amplifies confidence and lowers inhibition, which often leads to misfires. Spot the signal before the surge. Thought a girl was lip-smacking in your direction to get your attention, only to realize she had just put on fresh lipstick and you went over and got embarrassingly shot down? It happens. Cool your jets and your impulses.

Practice Self-Compassion

This is a process. You'll screw up. That's fine. Learn and move forward. Celebrate wins. Don't publicly beat yourself up. Self-awareness isn't self-loathing.

Seek Professional Help

If triggers feel opaque, get professional guidance. A skilled therapist can shorten the learning curve and help you regulate responses more effectively.

Mastering triggers lowers stress, restores agency, and stabilizes your system. With awareness and command, impulses lose their grip and sobriety gains ground.

"Know when to walk away, know when to run." - Kenny Rogers

Change Happens

Your world evolves whether you adapt or not. Time keeps marching. The smarter move is to face your future with change in mind. Embracing change consciously helps you navigate outside forces that may or may not support your goal of cutting back or quitting. Choose the change that moves you toward sobriety. Here are some tools to assist adapting to changes.

Anticipate Change

Most change isn't a clean, rip-the-bandage off moment, though it can be. Some prefer shock; many don't have the coping structure to shut the spigot off overnight. That's fine.

Think bigger than your current self. Set goals that feel just out of reach. If you land at 50%, you'll still surprise yourself, and that's progress. Visualize broadly, but respect the small wins. They stack.

You will falter. That doesn't make you weak. If you think elite performers didn't screw up along the way, you're delusional. Growth requires friction. Jung would call this confronting the shadow—meeting discomfort instead of pretending it doesn't exist. You are walking on the black mirror. You see only black, but the new life you are walking towards is you all along. Make moves that are uncomfortable *for you*. Life is for the living, and you need to live your best life. That looks different for everyone. It has nothing to do with money and everything to do with your own soul and peace.

Monitor Change

Review habits at a cadence you can sustain. Daily tracking works for some; weekly check-ins work for most. Monthly reviews often reveal the real shifts of both the mental and physical.

Each month, check for:

- Better sleep
- Some weight loss
- Clearer thinking, increased focus
- Improved conversations
- More presence with your kids or relatives

Did you drive home from work without stopping at the gas station for a 16oz tallboy or airplane shot of some tequila? That's a win. Track your progress for *you*. If you post progress online, fine—but don't rely on it. You already know how hollow that feedback loop is. You're competing with one person only: yourself. Only you care about yourself as much as you do. Read that again.

Adapt Quickly

Don't bite off more than you can chew. Going from five country club dirty martinis to zero overnight *can* happen—but relapse loves overconfidence. Solid progress beats heroics.

Assess honestly. Maybe switching from martinis to something lighter is a bridge. Ask a few trusted people for input. A real conversation about drinking less should get support. If it doesn't, stop discussing it with that person.

Act sooner rather than later. Change doesn't happen unless *you* do it, unless the system forces it on you. Jail is a lousy teacher. Trust us. Avoid that syllabus. Walking out of the drunk tank cell to the "personal property" window to collect your belongings after being booked for a DUI, only to meet your high school ex-girlfriend working at the desk—ugh.

Embrace the New You

BFI—Both Feet In. This is a mantra a good friend of ours has used consistently throughout his ever-changing life. Change isn't just reduction; it's replacement. Break patterns. Grow a beard for 2-3 months just to see how it goes - if you're a guy. If you are growing a beard as a woman, you might want to see a doctor about that. Change your hair in dramatic fashion. Wear the watch or earrings you bought as a sobriety marker. Eat new cuisine at new places. Explore new interests—*philes* are a good start (audiophile, cinephile, astrophile, javaphile, etc). Anything with the word 'phile' after it is a good start, except pedophile. Just don't become an insufferable expert overnight, wanting to school everyone on your newfound knowledge.

One shock for newly sober people: bar talk is mostly nonsense. Sober, you hear it clearly—and it's 99% gibberish bullshit. That's not judgment; it's awareness. You now have X-ray vision and hearing. Use it. The bee does not waste time trying to convince the fly that honey is better than shit. There's a reason sober people call drunks bar flies.

Choose environments that sharpen you, not dull you. If your friends are mixing booger sugar into the fun night, it gets way worse. Way worse. Their gibberish is amplified, and their heads look ready to explode. Get as far away from this as possible. Chicago Options Exchange or Wall Street–area NYC bars might still be a good proving ground for watching this kind of behavior unfold in real time. Nassau Bar, here we come. And when it unfolds, watch the fuck out.

Enjoy the Change

Reward yourself—but let the first reward be the change itself. Build on each win. Brick by brick.

The Art of Sober is a practice. It becomes a self-fulfilling prophecy when done daily, with fine adjustments along the way.

Some basic common practices include:

- Yoga or Hot Yoga, meditation
- Fishing and hunting; depends on where you live
- Gardening, potting, bonsai, vegetables
- Cooking, grilling, smoking, bread making, dessert making
- Hiking, biking, jogging, walking your dog longer
- Cat Ladying, fostering animals, pet shelter volunteerism
- Drawing and crafts, ceramics / pottery, woodworking
- Bowling, league sports, darts, fantasy leagues
- Mentoring, senior living volunteering, charity work

"Practice makes perfect" is the biggest line of bullshit ever. There is no making and reaching a permanent equilibrium. The *moment* might be perceived as perfect. The photograph might have captured a 'perfect' moment in time, but overall, nothing is continually perfect.

But you can get damn close. You're only as good as yesterday—and that's enough. Fall off. Get back on. Lose interest in a hobby. Find another. That's growth. If you are a Dad of younger boys and they are into video games, that might become a newfound interest of yours. That is ok. If you do not have kids, that might be a bit corny. If you never graduated from your Easy Bake little lightbulb oven into a real oven, well, we can't help that. If you never graduated from your Queasy Bake Cookerator, you are probably doomed and have way bigger problems than we can ever assist with.

You're allowed to mature. To outgrow things. To evolve. That's not failure—that's individuation.

Last Notes: Create Your Universe. Change and Enjoy Life Again
Create your universe. Domesticate it. You might take a pandeistic view of sobriety: you build a new sober universe and define the laws you choose to live by. Once that motion starts, alcohol loses its power to interfere with your day-to-day world or the natural order you're creating. You no longer live with the shadow. Let your sun shine so bright it leaves no shadows. No longer living with a head like a hole.

Alcohol no longer disrupts your unfolding life—one with a clear beginning to sobriety and no fixed end point. No grand destination required. The future without alcohol is simply *your being*. You, being you.

Being ready to change—and then evolving into that change—is the final summation of *The Art of Sober's Who Moved My Martini?*

Moving your martini. If you're not ready yet, that's fine. Life will continue as it is. What you put in is what you get out. No white knight is coming to save you. You are the artist. You have the tools. You are also the roadblock.

The Beginning of the End of Drinking
As a kickstart, may we suggest you try these activities:

Find your anthem
Scour your music services and pick a song that positively messages your journey and flips your mood on command. Make it your alarm, ringtone, brushing-teeth soundtrack—play it anywhere, anytime. Need a suggestion? Try "Roll with the Changes" by REO Speedwagon or "Solsbury Hill" by Peter Gabriel and turn it up. If someone asks why it's playing, tell them:

"It's my soundtrack."

Eat Alone—on Purpose

Pick a restaurant and eat there solo once every two weeks. Go at peak hours. Sit at a proper table in the middle, never the bar, never the corner, and never near the bathroom. Read a real paper book. Stay off your phone. This takes grit. You have grit; you just haven't needed it yet. Breakfast, lunch or dinner. Pick your daypart and go regularly.

What happens next surprises people: servers linger, bussers check in, strangers glance with approval. Why? Because confidence reads as sovereignty. Not drinking sharpens confidence in a way people chase but rarely achieve. You're doing it. You thrive in your own universe. Your bet on yourself is paying off in multiples. You're the 1%. The Irish Mafia. High voltage.

The Art of Sober mantra is simple:

"Once you feel too comfortable, it's time to change."

Soon this won't feel lonely, it will feel like *necessary solitude*. Mastery is sitting alone with nothing to do but think. It's hard. Bring a paper book if needed. Or stare outside at clouds. Watch water ripple. Notice shapes, reflections, movement. This is Jung's individuation at work—meeting yourself without distraction.

Choose One Solo Physical Practice.

Run, walk, swim, garden, build models, sketch, make a vision board—anything you can do alone. Keep it simple. Keep it affordable. Minimize electronics, avoid tv, unless you are now into film watching. If you're stuck, search online for "solo activities." Pick one and start.

Move quickly. Time gets in the way. If a "support group" distracts you from these practices, it isn't support. Remember: you don't have time, **time has you**.

Picture it: your anthem plays in your head. You walk into your favorite restaurant alone. People notice. You're calm. Centered. This follows your solo work. This is your universe, your sober universe.

You decide who coexists in it. No one can stop what's coming.

Practice this art. **Be sober. Feeling sober. Affirm sober.** When the feeling settles, the subconscious follows. Dwell in sobriety, and sobriety dwells in you. Release old wounds and regrets. Feed on gratitude. Change the assumption of who you are.

Do not judge yourself crossing the bridge. The old self must die. That death is symbolic, and necessary. It's the inheritance that sets you free.

Be sober. Then reintroduce only what fits your new life. Leave the old pieces on the dirt floor where they belong.

"I am and I was" becomes:

"I am and I am."

101 typical problems substance abuse causes

Here's a list of common problems that alcohol abuse can cause:

1. Physical health deterioration
2. Mental health disorders (e.g., depression, anxiety)
3. Relationship conflicts
4. Family dysfunction
5. Financial instability
6. Legal problems (e.g., DUIs, arrests)
7. Employment difficulties
8. Academic or educational setbacks
9. Social isolation
10. Decreased productivity
11. Increased risk of accidents or injuries
12. Risk of overdose or poisoning
13. Impaired cognitive function
14. Memory loss or blackouts
15. Liver damage (e.g., cirrhosis)
16. Heart problems (e.g., hypertension, heart disease)
17. Respiratory issues (e.g., lung damage)
18. Increased risk of cancer
19. Gastrointestinal problems (e.g., gastritis, ulcers)
20. Weakened immune system
21. Sexual dysfunction
22. Hormonal imbalances
23. Sleep disturbances
24. Nutritional deficiencies
25. Weight gain or loss
26. Skin problems (e.g., acne, premature aging)
27. Dental issues (e.g., gum disease, tooth decay)
28. Increased risk of infectious diseases (e.g., HIV, hepatitis)
29. Memory and cognitive impairments

30. Impaired judgment and decision-making
31. Difficulty concentrating or focusing
32. Mood swings or emotional instability
33. Aggressive or violent behavior
34. Paranoia or delusions
35. Hallucinations
36. Suicidal thoughts or behaviors
37. Self-harm or injuries
38. Decreased motivation or ambition
39. Loss of interest in hobbies or activities
40. Social withdrawal or isolation
41. Impaired social skills
42. Inability to maintain relationships
43. Codependency or enabling behaviors
44. Role confusion or identity issues
45. Lack of fulfillment or purpose
46. Feelings of guilt or shame
47. Low self-esteem or self-worth
48. Difficulty managing emotions
49. Emotional numbness or detachment
50. Sense of hopelessness or despair
51. Loss of spiritual connection or meaning
52. Engaging in risky or dangerous behaviors
53. Increased tolerance to substances
54. Withdrawal symptoms when not using substances
55. Cravings or urges to use substances
56. Obsessive thoughts about obtaining or using substances
57. Compulsive behaviors related to substance use
58. Loss of control over substance use
59. Inability to stop despite negative consequences
60. Denial or minimization of substance-related problems

61. Resistance to seeking help or treatment
62. Fear of judgment or stigma
63. Difficulty admitting or acknowledging the severity of the problem
64. Reluctance to change lifestyle or habits
65. Lack of awareness of available resources or support
66. Limited access to healthcare or treatment options
67. Financial barriers to treatment or rehabilitation
68. Lack of social support or encouragement
69. Fear of losing independence or autonomy
70. Concerns about confidentiality or privacy
71. Cultural or religious beliefs that discourage seeking help
72. Perceived lack of effectiveness or success of treatment programs
73. Fear of withdrawal symptoms or detoxification process
74. Skepticism or distrust of healthcare professionals or treatment providers
75. Fear of failure or relapse
76. Difficulty managing stress or coping with challenges
77. Lack of healthy coping mechanisms or stress management skills
78. Feelings of inadequacy or incompetence
79. Fear of losing relationships or support networks
80. Fear of facing consequences or responsibilities
81. Fear of confronting underlying emotional issues or trauma
82. Perceived lack of control or agency in one's life
83. Feelings of powerlessness or helplessness
84. Difficulty setting boundaries or asserting oneself
85. Fear of change or uncertainty
86. Resistance to accepting help or support from others
87. Fear of losing the perceived benefits of substance use
88. Reluctance to leave one's comfort zone or familiar surroundings
89. Concerns about the impact of treatment on one's daily life or routine

90. Fear of judgment or rejection from peers or social circles
91. Fear of losing one's sense of identity or purpose
92. Concerns about the impact of treatment on one's career or reputation
93. Fear of facing legal consequences or repercussions
94. Reluctance to confront or address underlying issues contributing to substance use
95. Fear of facing withdrawal symptoms or physical discomfort
96. Concerns about the financial cost of treatment or rehabilitation
97. Fear of relapse or setbacks during the recovery process
98. Reluctance to confront or acknowledge the impact of substance use on oneself or others
99. Concerns about the long-term implications of substance use on one's health, well-being, and future prospects
100. Fear of facing judgment, criticism, or stigma from others
101. Reluctance to take the first step toward seeking help or making changes in one's life

101 Benefits of not drinking alcohol:
1. Improved physical health
2. Enhanced mental clarity
3. Better sleep quality
4. Reduced risk of liver disease
5. Lowered blood pressure
6. Weight loss or weight management
7. Increased energy levels
8. Enhanced immune function
9. Reduced risk of certain cancers
10. Improved skin complexion
11. Better hydration
12. Reduced risk of heart disease
13. Improved digestive health
14. Reduced risk of stroke
15. Lowered risk of diabetes
16. Reduced risk of pancreatitis
17. Improved lung function
18. Better hormonal balance
19. Reduced risk of osteoporosis
20. Improved fertility
21. Better sexual function
22. Enhanced athletic performance
23. Stronger muscles and bones
24. Improved coordination and balance
25. Reduced risk of accidents and injuries
26. Better vision
27. Reduced inflammation
28. Enhanced detoxification processes
29. Strengthened immune system
30. Improved cardiovascular health

31. Reduced risk of dementia
32. Enhanced memory and cognition
33. Better mood regulation
34. Reduced anxiety levels
35. Increased resilience to stress
36. Better coping skills
37. Improved self-esteem
38. Enhanced social interactions
39. Deeper and more meaningful relationships
40. Increased emotional intimacy
41. Improved communication skills
42. Greater empathy and compassion
43. Enhanced creativity
44. Increased productivity
45. Better time management
46. Improved decision-making abilities
47. Enhanced problem-solving skills
48. Higher levels of motivation
49. Increased sense of purpose
50. Greater clarity of goals and aspirations
51. Improved career prospects
52. Enhanced financial stability
53. Better academic performance
54. Improved job satisfaction
55. Reduced absenteeism
56. Increased longevity
57. Enhanced quality of life
58. Better overall well-being
59. Increased self-awareness
60. Greater sense of authenticity
61. Improved self-discipline

62. Enhanced self-control
63. Reduced impulsivity
64. Greater sense of autonomy
65. Increased independence
66. Enhanced sense of freedom
67. Better decision-making in social situations
68. Reduced social anxiety
69. Improved social skills
70. Increased social confidence
71. Greater enjoyment of non-alcoholic activities
72. Deeper appreciation of life's simple pleasures
73. Enhanced mindfulness
74. Increased spiritual connection
75. Greater sense of inner peace
76. Reduced risk of addiction
77. Enhanced recovery from other addictions
78. Better management of co-occurring disorders
79. Reduced risk of relapse
80. Enhanced resilience to peer pressure
81. Better role modeling for others
82. Positive impact on family dynamics
83. Improved parenting skills
84. Better emotional regulation in relationships
85. Increased emotional stability
86. Reduced risk of domestic violence
87. Enhanced conflict resolution skills
88. Improved community engagement
89. Greater sense of social responsibility
90. Positive environmental impact
91. Reduced carbon footprint
92. Enhanced sense of connection to nature

93. Improved cognitive function in old age
94. Reduced healthcare costs
95. Lower insurance premiums
96. Increased financial savings
97. Reduced legal risks
98. Improved driving safety
99. Better public safety
100. Positive contribution to society
101. Overall, a happier, healthier, and more fulfilling life without alcohol

Bring *The Art of Sober* to your people

In a powerful 60–90 minute experience, we ditch the stale talk about alcohol and engage in a bold self-assessed performance review of people's relationship with it. The result: clarity, ownership, and the confidence to bet on themselves. Available as a signature keynote or customized for your organization.

Group settings large or small, from 1 person to 1000's, Ryan O'Day brings the message loud and f*ing clear about increasing performance, leadership, clarity, safety, and the tools needed for people to be a great artist of sober! Reach out today and connect with Ryan P. O'Day, he will leave your people wanting more.

www.TheArtofSober.com

Ideal engagements include;

- Corporate Leadership and Health & Wellness programs
  - Lunch & Learns (45-60 minute times)
  - Offsite meetings / retreats
  - 1 on 1 executive & C-Level recalibrations
  - OSHA oriented safety related subject matter
  - Sales / product kick off meetings
- Healthcare and medical conferences
- Trade show 30 minute sessions
- Recovery and mental health conferences
- University and High School presentations
- Professional sports organizations
- Insurance, OSHA, legal sponsored events
  - Risk, liability, workplace incidents
  - Workplace impairment
- High performance, entrepreneur, and sales events
  - Clarity, discipline, optimization
- Church groups